EA-6B Prowler

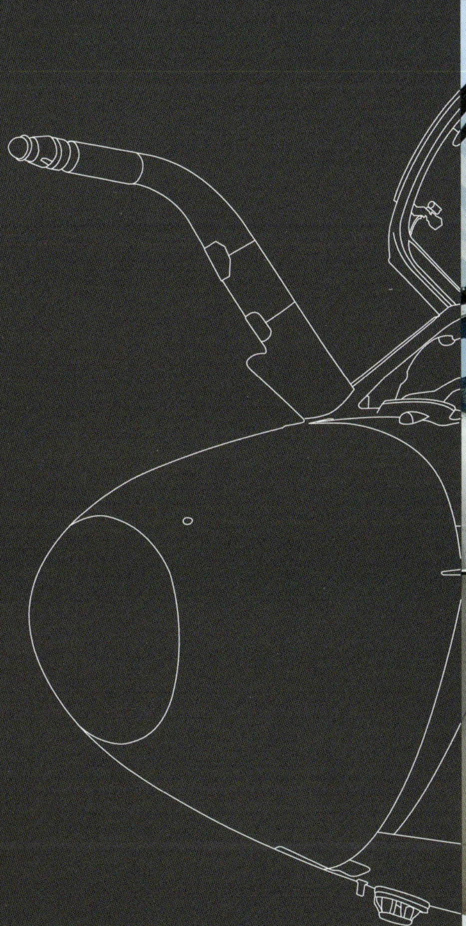

03

EA-6B
Prowler

Aerial warfare is much more than a matter of fighters and bombers, this is a lesson learned by the American forces during the Vietnam War. Disrupting enemy communications, radar systems and destroying them is an important part of aerial strategy, both in a defensive and offensive role. However, very few aircraft have been developped specifically for this role. For the US Navy and US Marines, this was the Grumman EA-6B Prowler. The Prowler is a four seat, two-engined jet that is used to jam enemy radar systems, gather radio intelligence and attack radar installations. The crew of the Prowler consists of a pilot and three Electronic Countermeasures Officers - ECMO's - with the one in the front seat also taking care of navigational tasks. The aircraft was developed from the Grumman Intruder, but has a longer fuselage and is packed with sensors and jamming equipment, either on the fuselage or in pods underneath the jet. The Navy started introducing the aircraft in 1971 - the first flight was in May 1968 - with the last Prowler taken out of service in 2019 from the US Marines.

While we had planned to make a book on the Prowler for a long time, it was the help and enthusiasm of Dave Chng that made things speed up, not in the least after his visit to the Frontiers of Flight Museum in Dallas, Texas to make some close-up photos of the aircraft. We also owe a big thank you to Akira Watanabe, who as a modeller knows exactly what we're looking for. Action photos made by Joe Copalman and Kevin Whitehead made the book very dynamic while the photos by Stephan Ortmann give you a glimps of the action on board American aircraft carriers. I really hope you'll enjoy the result!

Special thanks to these gentlemen, all aircraft enthusiasts:
Dave Chng, David Draycott, Philip Stevens, Akira Watanabe, Peter Anthoni, Stephan Ortmann, Joe Copalman, Kevin Whitehead, US Navy, US Marines, US Air Force and Gunter Geens.

Photo: MCSS Chelsy Alamina, US Navy

An EA-6B Prowler of VAQ-209 "Star Warriors" is taxiing with wings folded towards its parking spot. Behind it, another Prowler is taxiing, but with the wings unfolded. With a wingspan of 16 meter and limited room on the deck of an aircraft carrier, foldable wings are a necessity. Although the EA-6B is a large aircraft, it is an agile one too, sometimes doing some impressive manoeuvres, even at low level, as you will see in this book. It is powered by a pair of Pratt & Whitney J52-P-408A turbojet engines, giving just over 20,000 lbs of thrust and enabling the aircraft to fly at speeds of up to 1, 048 km/h.

The Grumman EA-6B Prowler was developped from the A-6 Intruder
and is basically a 4-seat modification of the latter. Grumman built 170
of the type and although only one type was developped, it doesn't mean
that there weren't any updates during the 48 years that the type has
been operational. The modifications were mostly in terms of avionics,
radar or jamming capabilities, with hardly any external differences. The
updates were indicated by the abreviation ICAP - Improved Capability
- of which several were developped. ICAP II was a development of the
Prowler that introduced modernisation of the external pods, avionics
and navigation systems. With this modification, the Prowler was
also capable of carrying the HARM anti-radiation missile, as seen
underneath the port wing in the photo to the right. All surviving aircraft
were upgraded to the ICAP II standards. Newly introduced Prowlers
with these capabilities were known as "Block 86" aircraft and could
be recognised by three antennas on the spine and under the forward
fuselage. A limited ICAP III modification was presented near the end of
the service life of the aircraft.

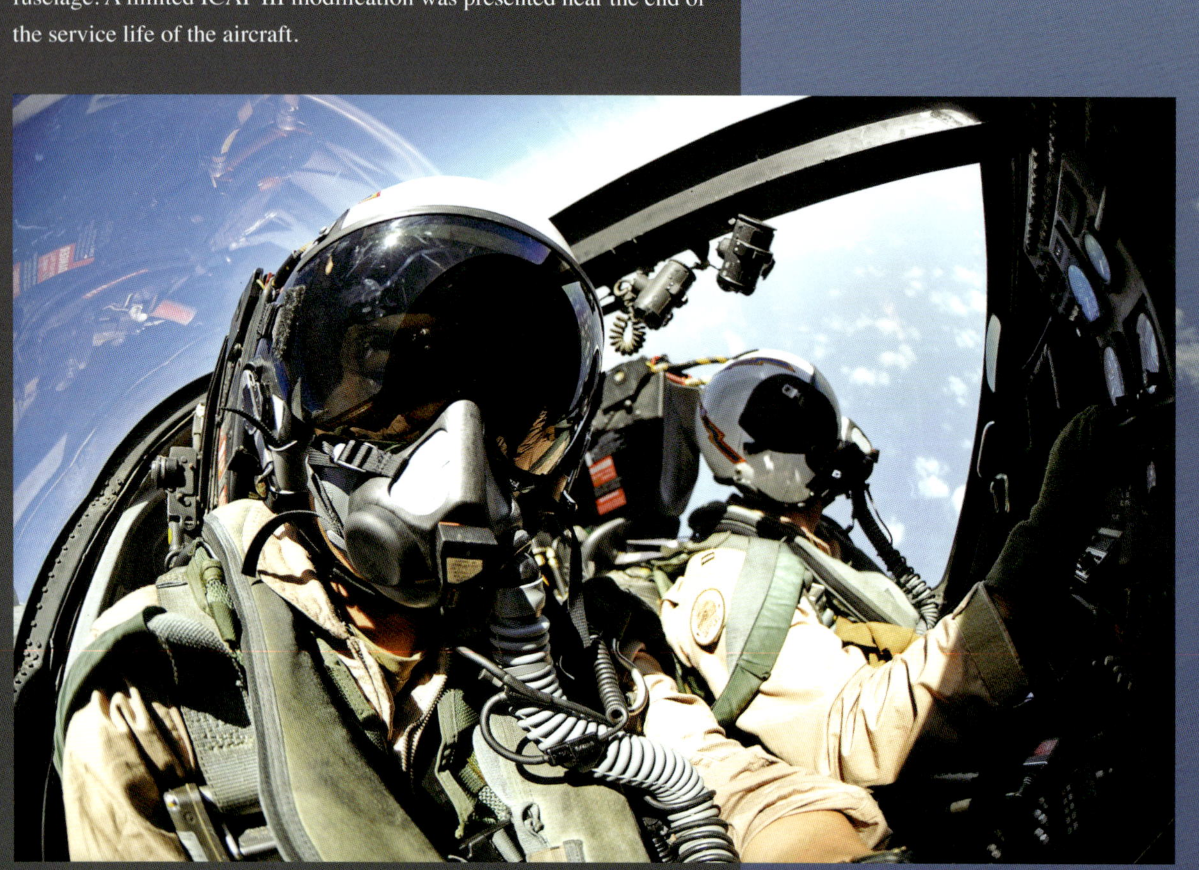

A Prowler is about to be refuelled by
a KC-135 Stratotanker. Underneath
the port wing, an AGM-88 HARM is
loaded. Notice how the cover panels of
the starboard wing folding mechanism
are missing.

507 ARW
137 ARW

Top: A Prowler is hooked up to the launch shuttle and the deck crew signals that it is ready for take off. Compared to the A-6 Intruder, the forward fuselage of the Prowler was lengthened by 1,37 meter to accommodate the extra 2 seats and avionics equipment.

Above and left: These photos show the lower part of the forward fuselage. In front of the nose landing gear, a large blade antenna, a smaller antenna and a navigation light are located.

Right: This photo, taken during Red Flag Alaska in 2014, held at Eielson Air Force Base, shows Lt. Candice Nunley, an EA-6B Prowler pilot from VAQ-142 "Gray Wolves", entering her aircraft. The unit, which today flies the EA-18G Growler, is based at Naval Air Station Whidbey Island in Washington state. Notice the folded down entrance step on the side of the fuselage and the red painted interior of the bay and door. Look at all the chipping at the front end of the In-flight Refuelling probe.

Below: In front of the windscreen on the port side, a red refuelling probe light is located.

Photo: Akira Watanabe

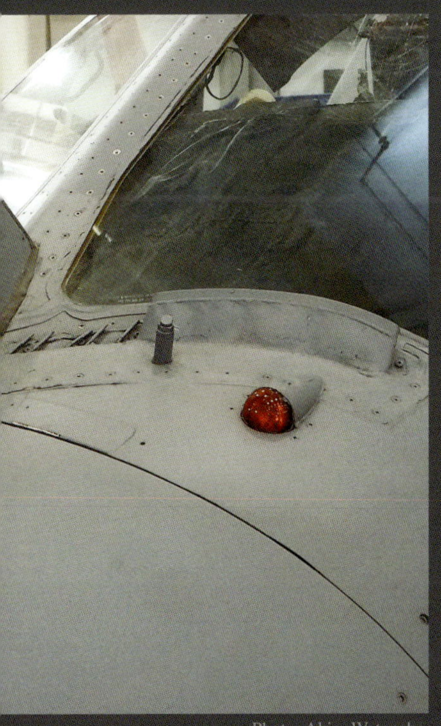

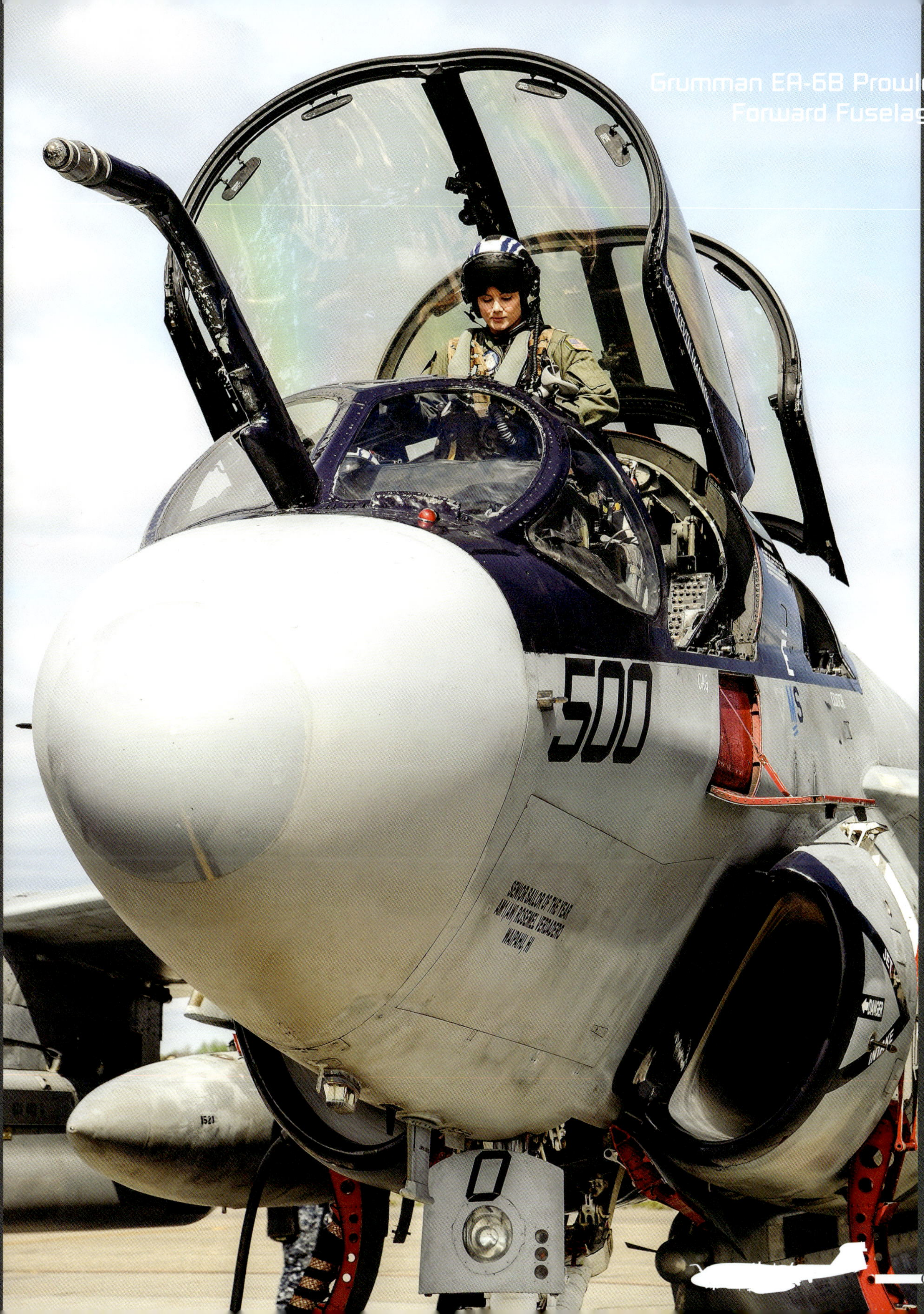

Photo: Sr Airman Zachary Perras, USAF

Left: An EA-6B Prowler assigned to the "Gray Wolves" - VAQ-142 - is about ready to launch from the flight deck of the USS Nimitz during Operation Enduring Freedom. Deck crew are doing a final check to see if the gear is hooked up properly to the launch shuttle and the holdback bar. On the forward fuselage, immediately aft of the radome, a pitot tube is located on either side of the fuselage. Look at the position of the navigation light and antennas underneath the nose.

Below: the In-Flight Refuelling probe located in front of the windscreen in detail. The housing at the base of it holds the receiver antenna of the AN/ALQ-126 Noise Deception Jammer. Like every other US Navy jet, the Prowler is refuelled in the air by tankers equipped with a refuelling basket.

Above: The In-Flight Refuelling probe of the Prowler is offset to starboard, making sure that the pilot, who sits in the left seat, has a clear view when flying. Notice the Rain removal and de-icing system located in front of the pilot's position.

Above right: A close-up of the large antenna underneath the nose of the Prowler, with the "Do Not Paint" stencil written upside-down on it.

Right: The port forward fuselage of an EA-6B Prowler of the US Marines. Notice the large avionics door and the entrance step located above it. This step can be lowered by simply pushing a pair of buttons on it. The boarding ladder is located on the aircraft's air intake. Notice the very cool looking VMFA-115 "Silver Eagles" F/A-18 Legacy Hornet in the back!

Photo: Dave Chng

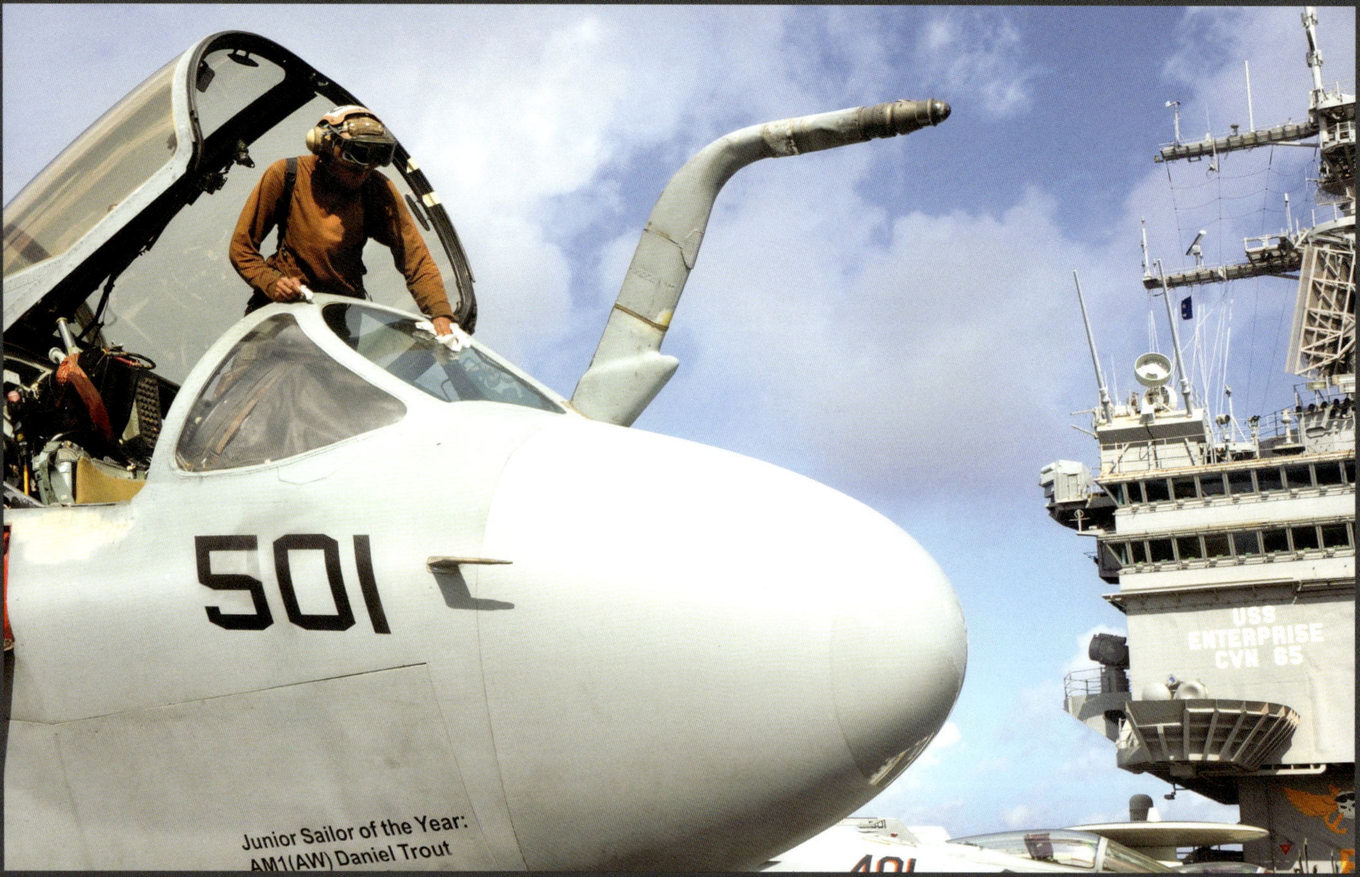

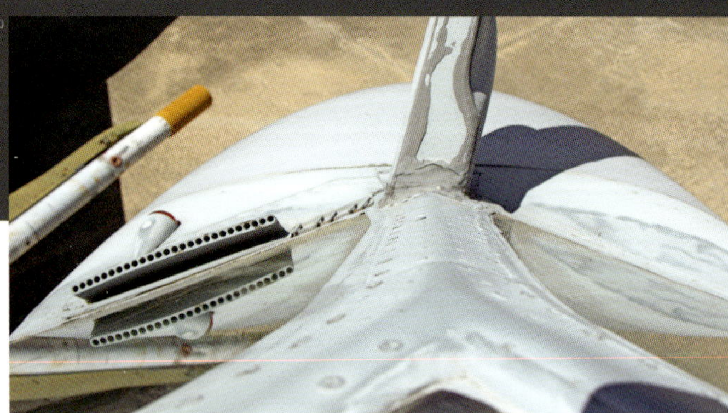

Left: A Plane Captain is cleaning the windscreen of a Prowler, making sure visibility is optimal during flight. Notice the bulge on the In-Flight Refuelling probe, housing the antenna of the AN/ALQ-126 Jammer. A reinforcement plate has been attached to the probe. Notice the pitot tube and the canvas covering the forward instruments.

Photo: Dave Chng

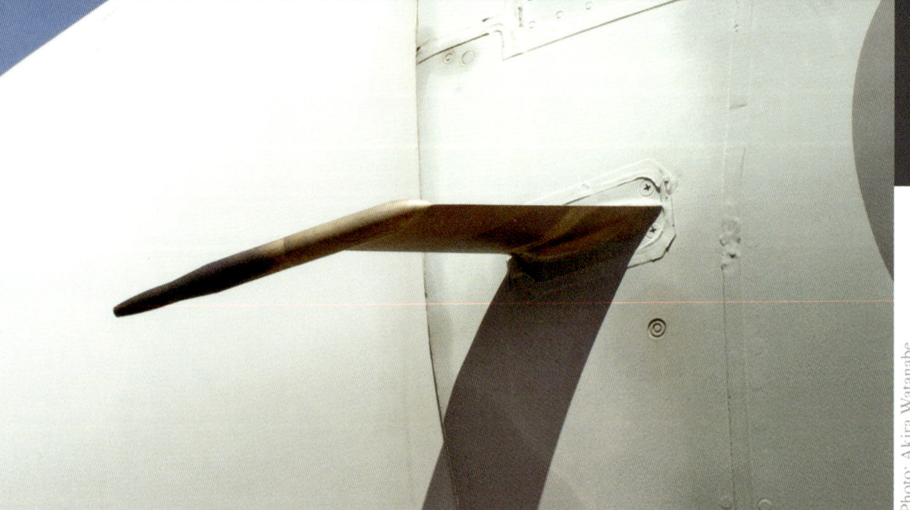

Above: Standing in the front cockpit and looking down over the windscreen, this is what you see. In front of the pilot's seat, air pressure vents make sure rain is removed to ensure optimal vision. Notice the angle of the in-flight refuelling probe's base.

Photo: Akira Watanabe

Right: Steam from the catapults is blowing over the deck of the USS Nimitz in the summer of 2013 when a Prowler of VAQ-142 "Gray Wolves" is being directed to one of the bow catapults during operations in the Gulf of Oman. Look at the details of the port forward fuselage and the lowered leading edge slat.

Photo: PO 3rd Class Raul Moreno, US Navy

Photo: Akira Watanabe

Photo: Akira Watanabe

Left: In 2008, this EA-6B of VAQ-137 "Rooks" received this attractive nose art, when flying of the USS Enterprise. The unit continued to fly the Prowler until 2012, after which it transitionned to the E A-18G Growler.

Photo: Stephan Ortmann

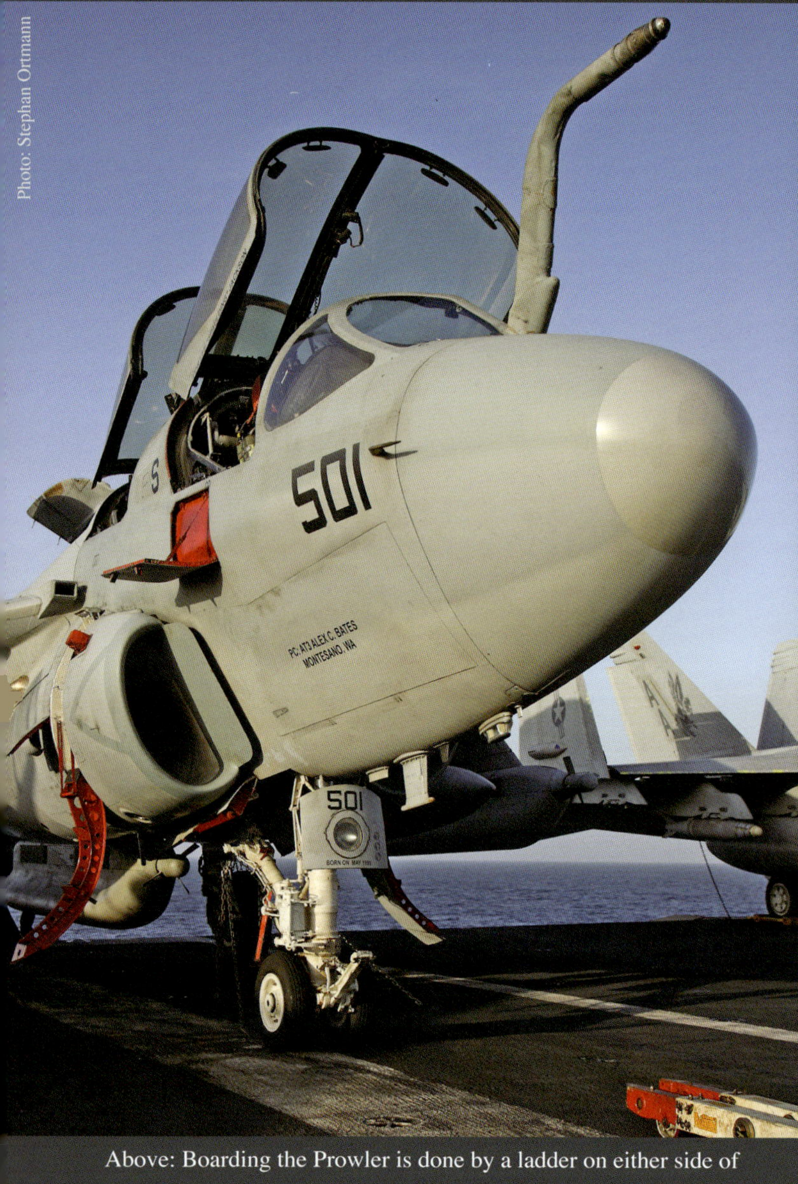

Above: Boarding the Prowler is done by a ladder on either side of the fuselage, located outside the air intake. The pilot and the ECMO - Electronic Countermeasures Operator - in the front, step onto the platform located forward of the air intake to get into the cockpit.

Right: A fantastic overall view of the port forward fuselage of the Prowler. See where the ladder and steps are located?

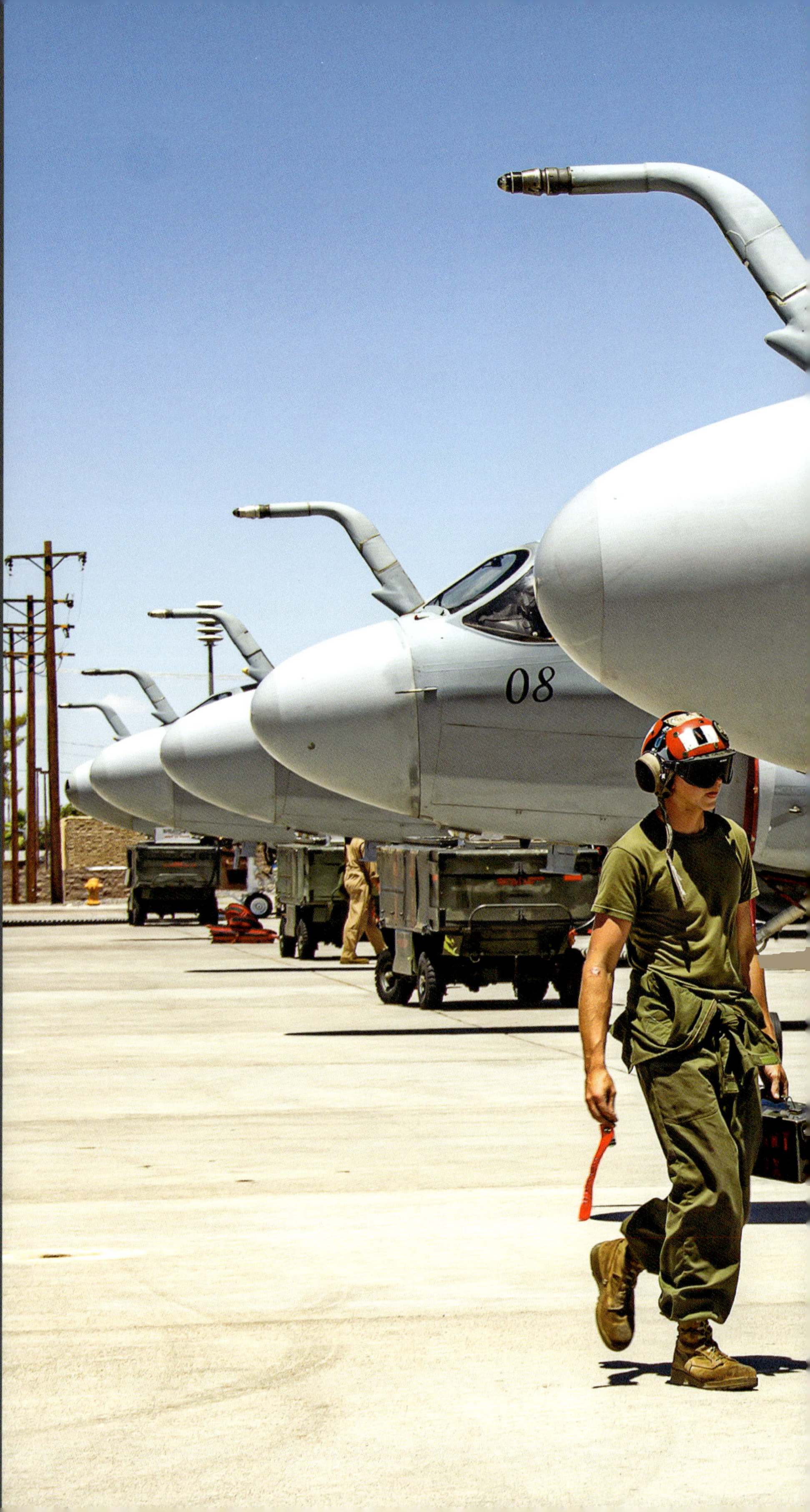

Grumman EA-6B Prowler
Forward Fuselage
09
JET
DANGER
INTAKE
Photo: Dave Craig

Above: When parked on the flight deck, usually, a tow bar is connected to the nose wheel. Look at the indication underneath the aircraft's index: "Give 'em hell!".

Right: Cleaning the canopy, standing on the folded down platform. Look at the gold-brown shade of the canopy glass.

Photo: Philip Stevens

Photo: Stephan Ortmann

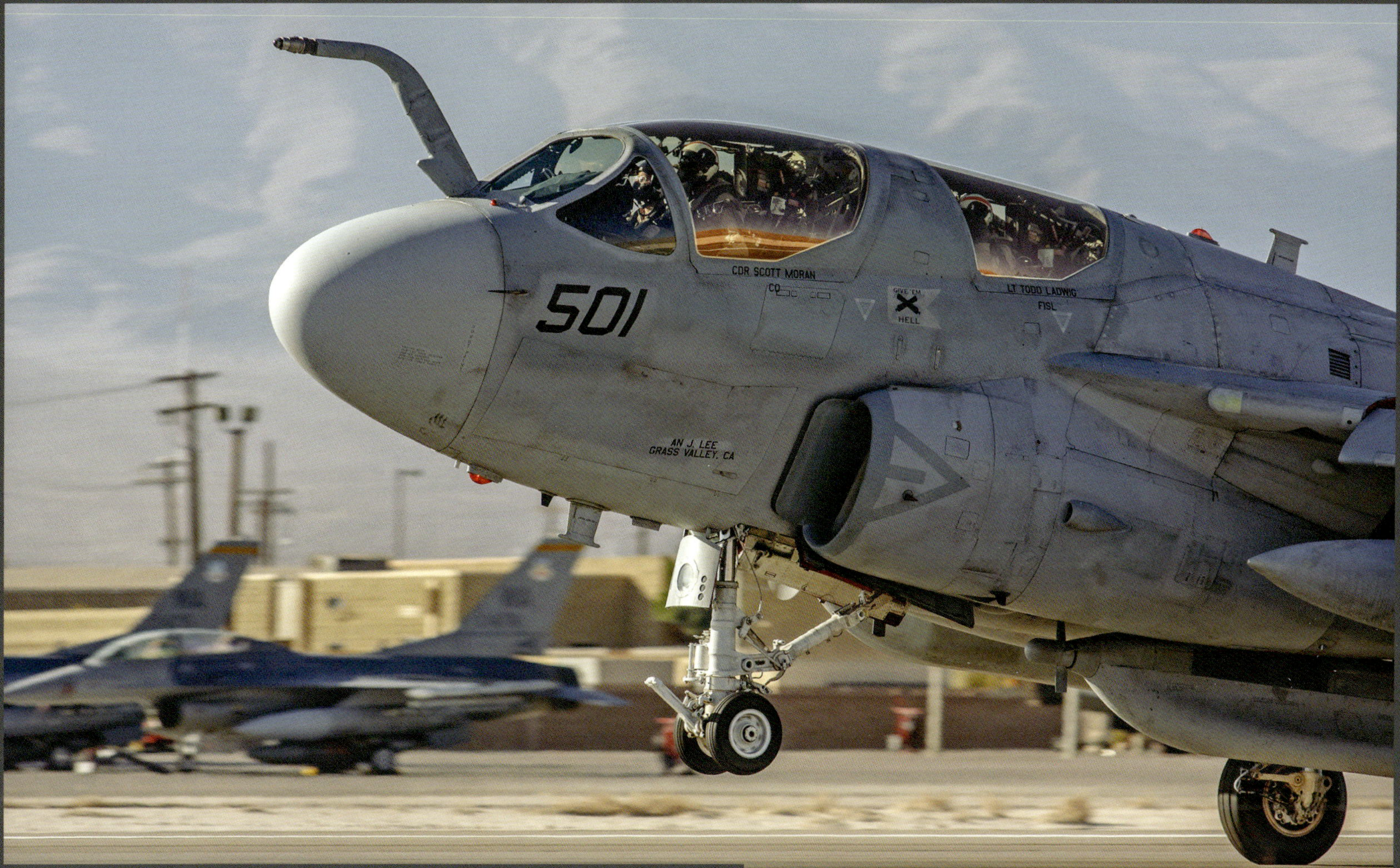

Photo: Philip Stevens

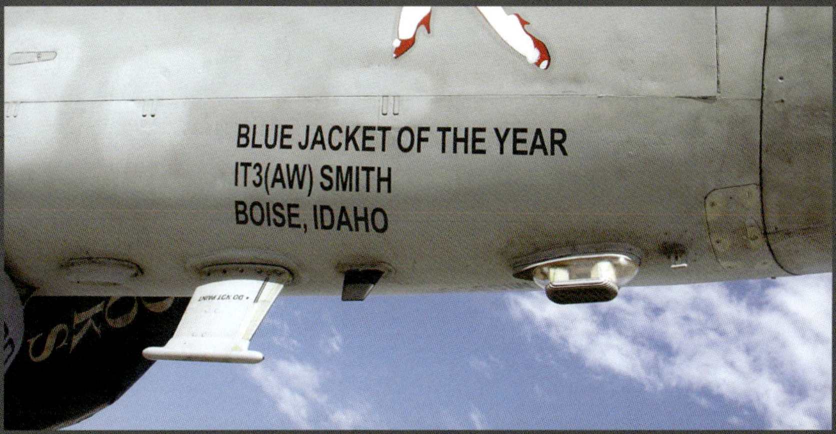

Photo: Akira Watanabe

Above: An EA-6B Prowler is landing back at Nellis Air Force Base during a Red Flag training flight. Notice how the forward main gear doors are closed; they close automatically when the aircraft is powered up. Look at the "Do Not Paint" stencil on the radome and the old-style red navigation light underneath the nose and on top of the fuselage.

Left: A close-up of the equipment located underneath the nose of the EA-6B, with the more recent navigation light - compare it to the photo above. Behind it is a small black UHF/VHF antenna in front of the large TACAN antenna, part of the aircraft's navigation system. More aft is the AN/APN-154 Radar Tracking beacon.

Photo: Joe Copalman

How about this for a close-up made during an air-to-air photoshoot? This awesome photo by Joe Copalman shows so many interesting parts of the starboard forward fuselage of the Prowler. Aft of the radome is one of the pitot tubes - another one is located on the port side. Look at the air intake and the fixed splitter plate to the front of it. Notice the Angle of Attack probe on top of the air intake; when the aircraft is on the ground, this part is protected by a forward folding cover, immediately behind it. On the starboard side, below the aft cockpit, a rectangular air intake is located, providing air for the airconditioning system. Look at the navigation lights and the round GPS antenna on top of the fuselage. I really like the weathered look of this Prowler.

Right: Three Prowlers, neatly parked next to each other on the flight deck of an aircraft carrier, are being cleaned prior to a flight during Operation Enduring Freedom. If you look closely, you see a lot of details, such as the folded down step, entrance ladder and even cockpit details. Not seen very often on the flight deck, are the remove before flight tags over the inspection panel, next to the boarding ladder housing. Notice the shades of grey and the weathering on the fuselage, typical of US Navy jets.

Left: This Prowler was seen during a Red Flag exercise at Nellis Air Force Base. Look at all the mission marking on the forward fuselage, a proof of operational missions in the Middle East.

There are quite a few interesting details in this photo, such as the open panel in front of the main landing gear and the open access panel on the engine cowling. The forward main landing gear doors close when the aircraft is powered up. This photo also shows that the crew in the front cockpit each have two rear-view mirrors.

Photo: Kevin Whitehead

Above: This Prowler was assigned to VX-23 "Salty Dogs", based at Naval Air Station Patuxant River in Maryland, which is a Test and Evaluation unit. The aircraft is used to test new avionics systems, jamming equipment or even weapons such as the AGM-88 HARM anti-radiation missile. Currently, the unit tests aircraft and equipment on the Super Hornet, F-35C or MQ-25 drone to name but a few.

Right: The forward cockpit canopy, seen from the starboard side.

Photo: Akira Watanabe

Below: A Yellow Shirt directs an EA-6B Prowler assigned to VAQ-134 "Garudas" on the flight deck of the aircraft carrier USS George H.W. Bush . It is August 2014 and somewhere in the Persian Gulf. U.S. Central Command directed targeted airstrikes against ISIS terrorists operating in Iraq and the Prowlers were used to jam the communication capabilities on the ground. Notice the large cover over the wing folding mechanism in this photo and the battered In-Flight Refuelling probe.

Photo: MC3 Joshua Card, US Navy

21

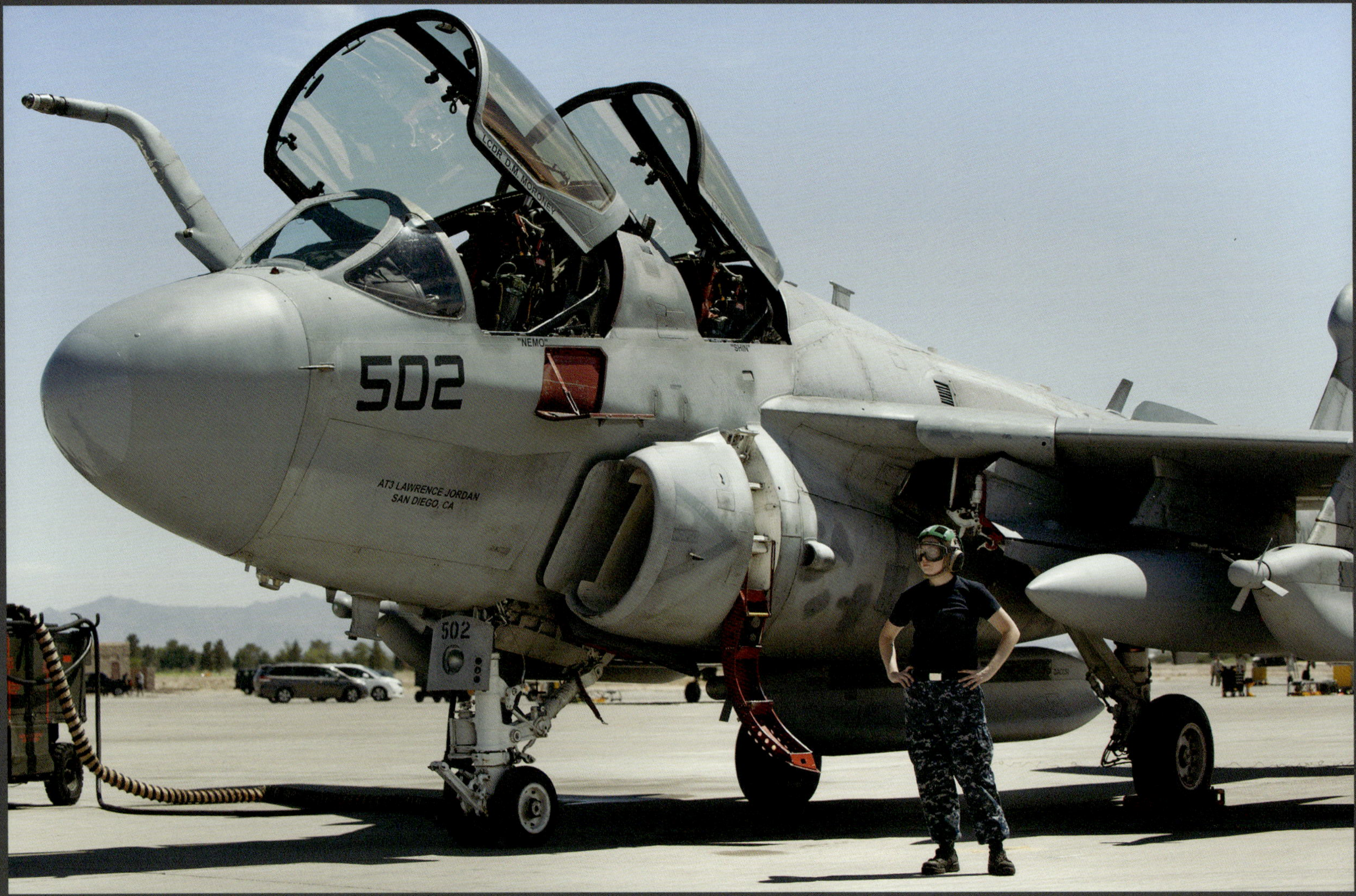

The EA-6B Prowler is powered by a pair of Pratt & Whitney J52-P-408A turbojet engines. The air for the engines is provided by two air intakes located halfway underneath the triangular shaped fuselage. To the front of the air intakes, a fixed splitter plate is located. The distance created between the fuselage and air intakes ensures that no turbulant air coming from the fuselahe enters te engines. Each of the air intakes houses a crew boarding ladder, which is simply folded down. I like the pose of the ground crew in the photo above. I imagine that she's thinking: "Why is it always me that has to wait on the others ...".

Right: A look in the port air intake with the compressor blades of the engine at the end. The interior of the air intake is painted gloss white.

Photo: Akira Watanabe

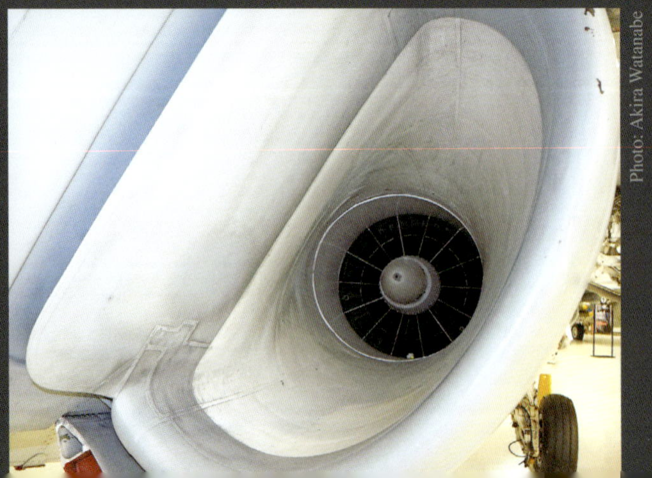

A fantastic head-on shot of a Prowler about to
refuel. Look at the distance between the air intakes
and the fuselage. Notice the square air conditioning
air intake at the root of the starboard wing. This
Prowler is loaded with a pair of external fuel tanks
- notice the the empty outboard pylons.

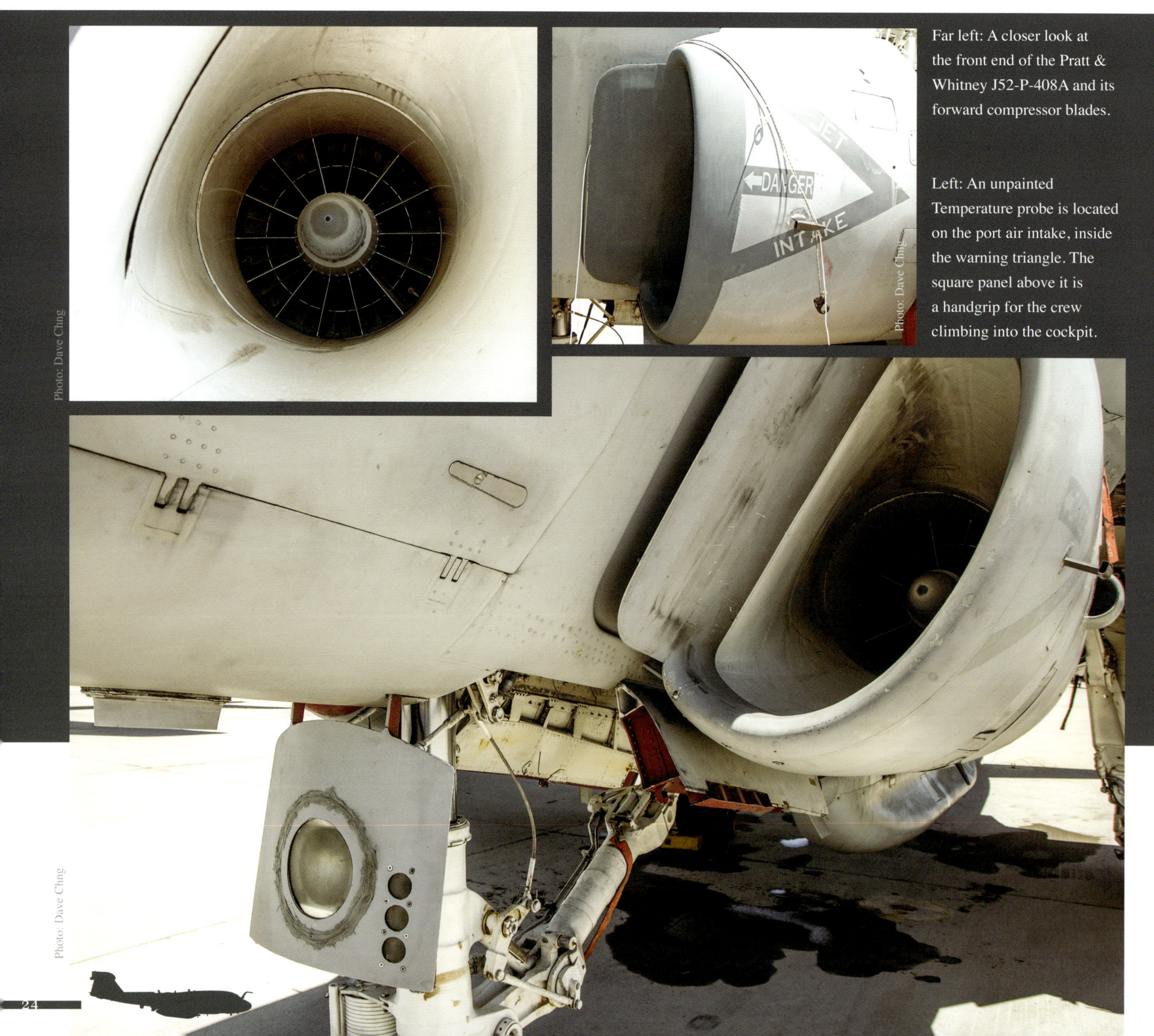

Far left: A closer look at the front end of the Pratt & Whitney J52-P-408A and its forward compressor blades.

Left: An unpainted Temperature probe is located on the port air intake, inside the warning triangle. The square panel above it is a handgrip for the crew climbing into the cockpit.

Photo: Dave Chng

Photo: Dave Chng

Photo: Dave Chng

Right: The port air intake with an intake cover. The cords in the photo are from covers over the aircraft, to protect it from the sun.

Below: A close-up of the starboard air intake interior. Look at the compressor blades and the two temperature probes.

Photo: Dave Chng

Photo: Dave Chng

Photo: Dave Chng

Photo: L-Cpl. Liam D. Higgins, USMC

Above: Two U.S. Marine Corps Grumman EA-6B Prowlers assigned to VMAQ-2 "Death Jesters" fly off the coast of North Carolina in February of 2019. VMAQ-2 was conducting its last flights prior to their deactivation just a month later. VMAQ-2 was established as Marine Composite Squadron 2 - VMC-2- on 15 September 1952 and was the last squadron to fly the EA-6B Prowler. The jet in the front is looking really smart with the black and red accents.

Left: Air intake covers and jet exhaust covers in close-up. I guess they've seen better days... Look at the black material on the inside of the engine covers.

Photo: Dave Chng

Photo: Dave Chng

Right: This photo gives a good view on the structure of the air intake, both from the outside and the inside.

Below, right: A close-up of the port air intake. To the right of the boarding steps, you can see two panels one above the other: the top one houses the Electrical Power Systems check, the one below is for the Ground Power Circuit Braker panel. The large panel behind it with the additional intake, has a rectangular panel which can be opened with two quick release buttons. Behind it is a check for the hydraulic system.

Photo: Dave Chng

Photo: Dave Chng

Photo: Dave Chng

Left: The exterior of the starboard air intake. To the right of the boarding steps, you can see the forward folded cover over the Angle of Attack probe. To the left of the ladder, some open panels can be seen. In front of the air scoop is the electrical ground power hook-up. Below and aft of this point is the hook-up for the External Power Unit for compressed air. The Prowler doesn't have self-starting engines. The hook up starts the starboard engine, which in turn starts the port engine.

Right & above right: Also on the starboard side of the aircraft, is the single point refuelling point. No cover over this point though. On the other hand, it allows the refuelling crews on the deck of the aircraft carrier to quickly refuel the jet. Look at the airscoop underneath the intake and the blade antenna next to it.

Above: The Angle of Attack probe located on the starboard air intake. Behind it is the folded back cover for it. You don't want to fall on this probe when entering the aircraft.

Photo: Dave Ching

Photo: US Navy

Photo: Dave Chng

Above: A Green shirt shows the weight of the aircraft to the flight crew, which is about to take off from the carrier. The wings have to be lowered first, though.

Left: Looking more aft on the starboard side of the aircraft, the gold-metal coloured part is the exhaust of the air conditioning system. The air condition is used to cool both the cockpits and the many avionics systems of the Prowler. Notice the external power panel and the start access panels. All these panels can be opened by simple quick release buttons.

Photo: Akira Watanabe

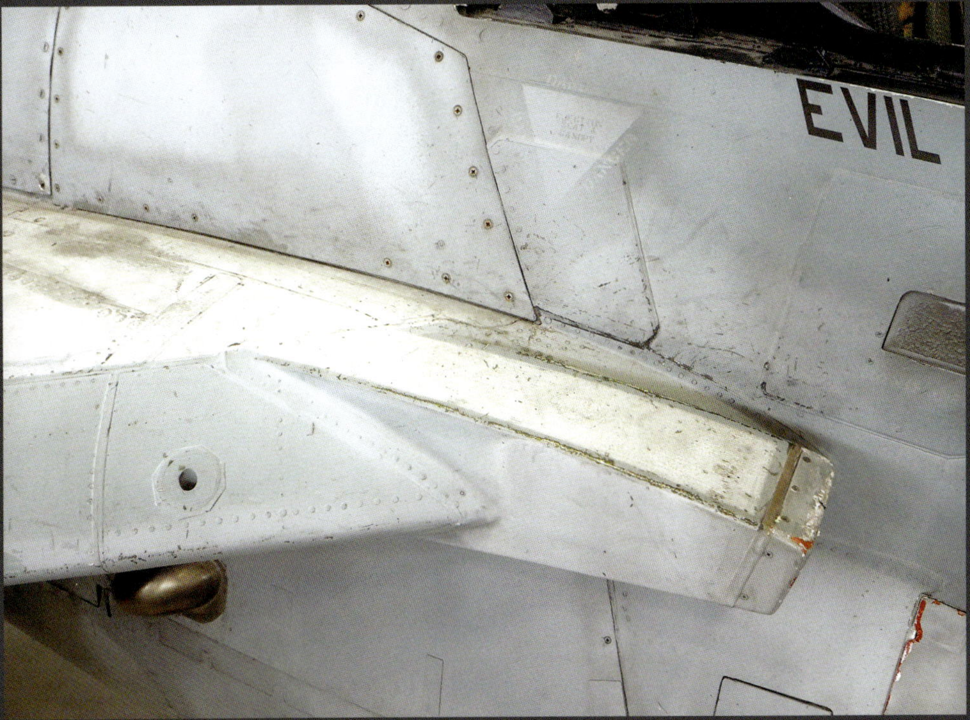

Left: Next to the aft cockpit on the starboard side of the aircraft, a small rectangular air intake is located, providing air to the Air conditioning cooling system. This is a view of the area seen from above. Below: The same area, seen from the ground. Notice the AOA probe.

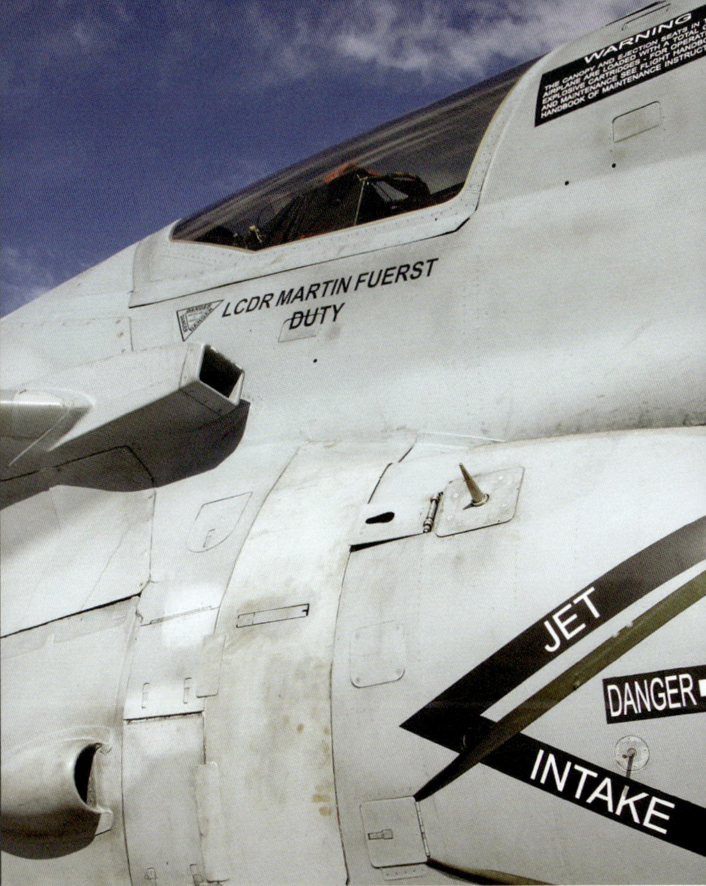

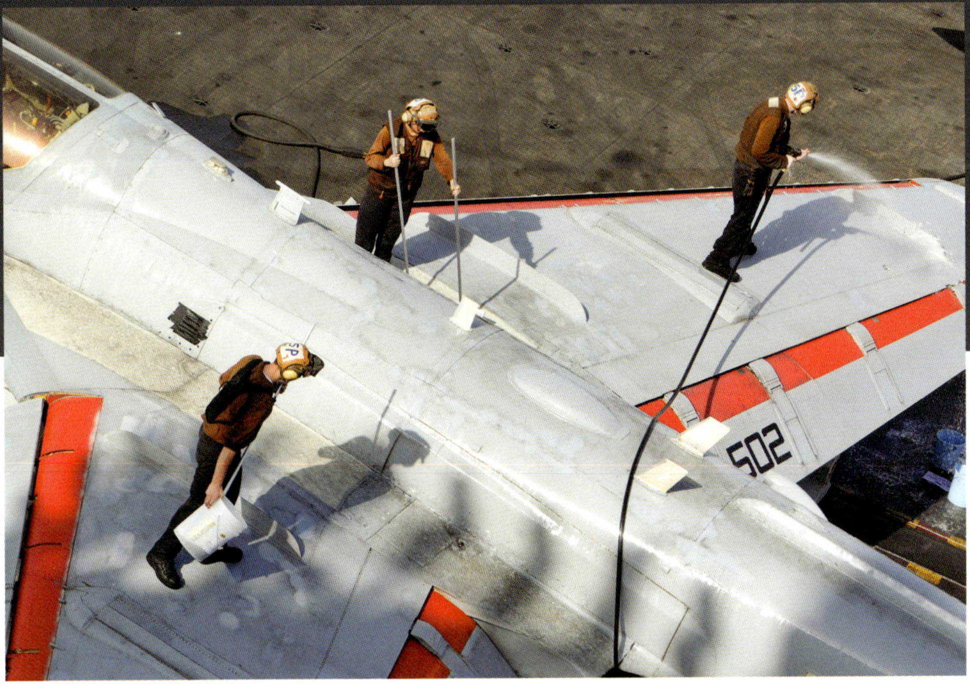

Left: The wings and the upper fuselage of a Prowler of VAQ-140 "Patriots" is getting cleaned by deck crew of the unit. Dirt and salt need to be washed off, but before doing so, openings on the fuselage have to be taped over. Notice the three white blade antennas on the fuselage, which were installed to update the aircraft to ICAP II standards.

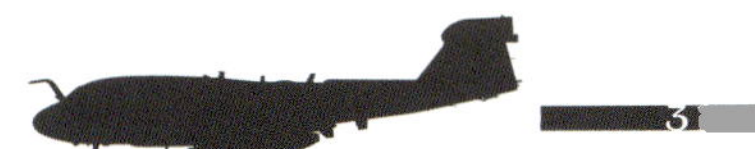

Above: An EA-6B Prowler assigned to Marine Tactical Electronic Warfare Squadron 3 taxis toward the runway in the fall of 2015, at Osan Air Base in South Korea. The unit participated in exercise Pacific Thunder 15-02, which lasted about 2 weeks. The unit, called the "Moon Dogs" sport a couple of angry looking beasts on the fuselage, one on the nose, another on the rudder. I really like the one on the rudder, but I can't help to think of Ramsay Bolton from Games of Thrones. Nasty guy...

Photo: Dave Chng

Photo: Dave Chng

Photo: Dave Chng

Some close-up shots of the port boarding ladder. It takes seven steps to get into the back cockpit. The pilot and Navigator/ECMO have to step onto a foldable platform before they can get into the front cockpit. Best make sure not to slip, it is quite a height to fall from. Notice that a stowage area is located immediately above the red painted steps. Look at the hand-holds on the steps and in the fuselage to the left of the ladder. Like with all US Navy aircraft, the insides of moving parts, such as ladders, slats, flaps, speed brakes, gear doors and access panels are painted red. The bays themselves are usually painted gloss white, making it easier to spot leaks.

Photo: Dave Chng

Above: Basking in the Nevada sun, a pair of Prowlers from VMAQ-4 "Seahawks" are ready for another training mission. Look at the different shades of the panels on the electronics pod on top of the vertical tail.

Climbing into the Prowler

Right, so getting into the Prowler takes a little climbing: with the access ladder lowered, it takes seven steps to get into the aft cockpit. Crew for the front cockpit then need to take a big step onto the folded down platform, seen in the photo to the right. Look at the chipped framing next to the ejection seat, but we'll get to that in detail in the cockpit chapter of the book.

Photo: Dave Chng

Right: The port fuselage seen from behind. Look at all the antennas on top of the fuselage and the jammer pods underneath the wings and fuselage. Notice that the shape of the one on the centerline hardpoint is different. The RAM air turbine is deployed near the wing root. Have a look at the wing fences on both inner and outer parts of the wing.

Below: A Prowler is being refuelled on the deck of a US aircraft carrier. Notice the tow bar attached to the nose wheel.

Below right: The lowered ladder seen from underneath the jet. Look at the handle.

Photo: Dave Chng

Photo: US Navy

Photo: Dave Chng

Photo: Kevin Whitehead

Above: During one of the Weapons and Tactics Instructor courses held at MCAS Yuma, this Prowler of VMAQ-2 "Death Jesters" wore a spectacular partially digital camouflage. The squadron, which was decommissioned in 2019, was activated in 1952, then flying the AD-5 Skyraider.

Right: How about this for an awesome photo? During September and October 2017, VMAQ-2 participated in Weapons and Tactics Instructor - WTI - course 1-18, held at MCAS Yuma in Arizona. In past courses, the Marine EA-6B community sent Prowler pilots and ECMOs to the course to become weapons and tactics instructors in their assigned squadrons, with the last Prowler WTIs graduating during WTI 2-17 in April and May 2017. During WTI 1-18, the "Death Jesters" provided EW assets for other platforms during the course, while conducting additional training for the squadron's final deployment to the Middle East.

78
46
VMAQ-2
MARINES

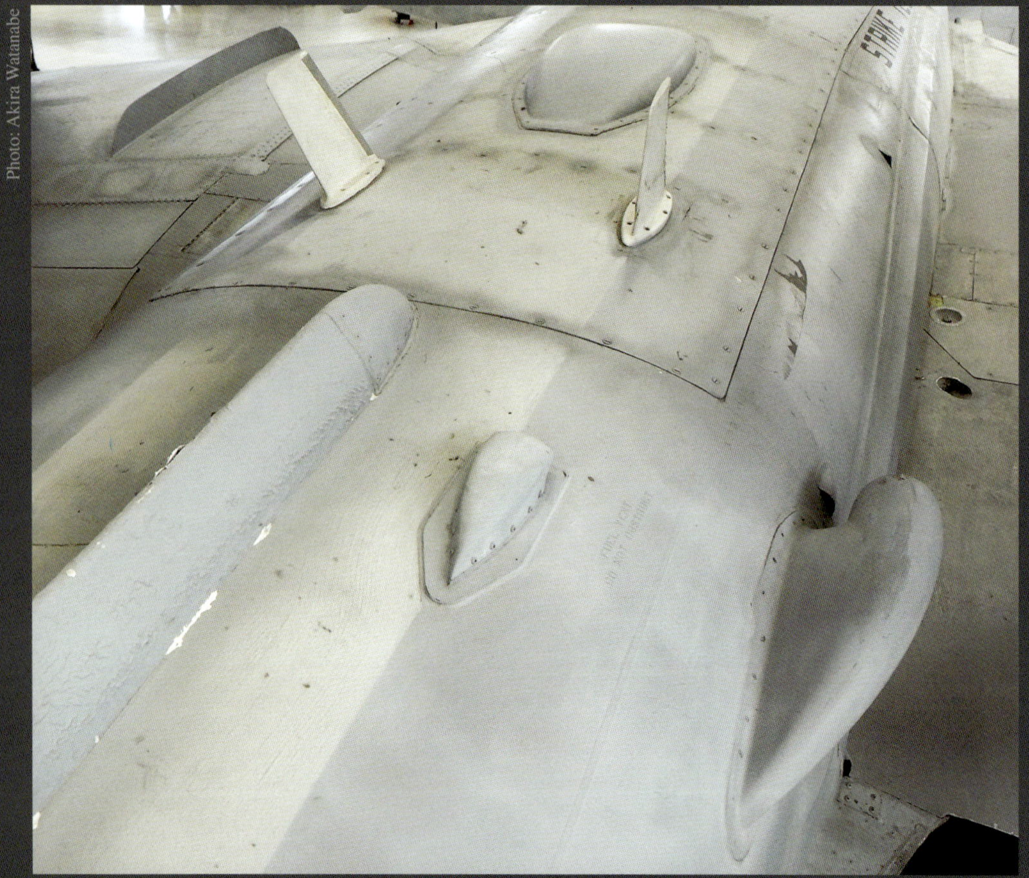

Above: The oval shaped antenna on top of the fuselage is the AN/ARA-50 UHF Automatic Direction Finder, which is an additional navigation system, guided by radio stations on the ground.

Above: The top of the fuselage, seen from the back towards the nose of the aircraft. The two white blade antennas are part of the AN/ARC-182 radio equipment, which was introduced with the ICAP II upgrade. ICAP stands for Improved Capability. Look how far forward the base of the vertical tail extends; it contains the AN/ARC-105 HF antenna.

Right: to the starboard side of the aft fuselage, a large air conditioning intake is located, providing cooled air for the electronic equipment of the aircraft. The scoop above it, near the base of the vertical tail, is a fuel vent. The top of the aircraft's spine is painted in a lighter shade of grey, except for the antennas.

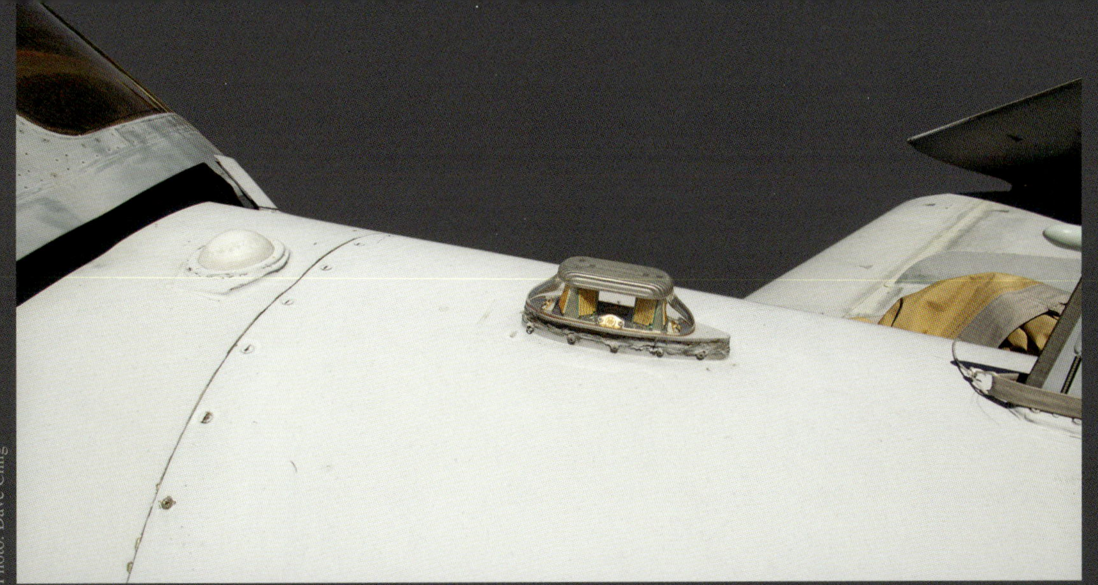

Photo: Dave Chng

Left: The navigation light on top of the spine of the Prowler. Notice the round GPS antenna located in front of it, immediately aft of the canopy. The GPS was introduced in the Block 89 aircraft.

Below: A great view of a Prowler being readied for another mission. Look at the wing tip of the aircraft with the formation strips and the close speed brakes. On the top part of it, static dischargers are located.

Photo: Joe Copalman

Above & left: The walk-ways on top of the wing roots on the starboard side of the aircraft. Notice the circuit breaker vent near the front of the fuselage fairing. This vent can also be found on the port side of the fuselage.

Above: A clear view of the engine compartment on the port side of the aircraft. Notice the leading edge of the wing with the dog tooth.

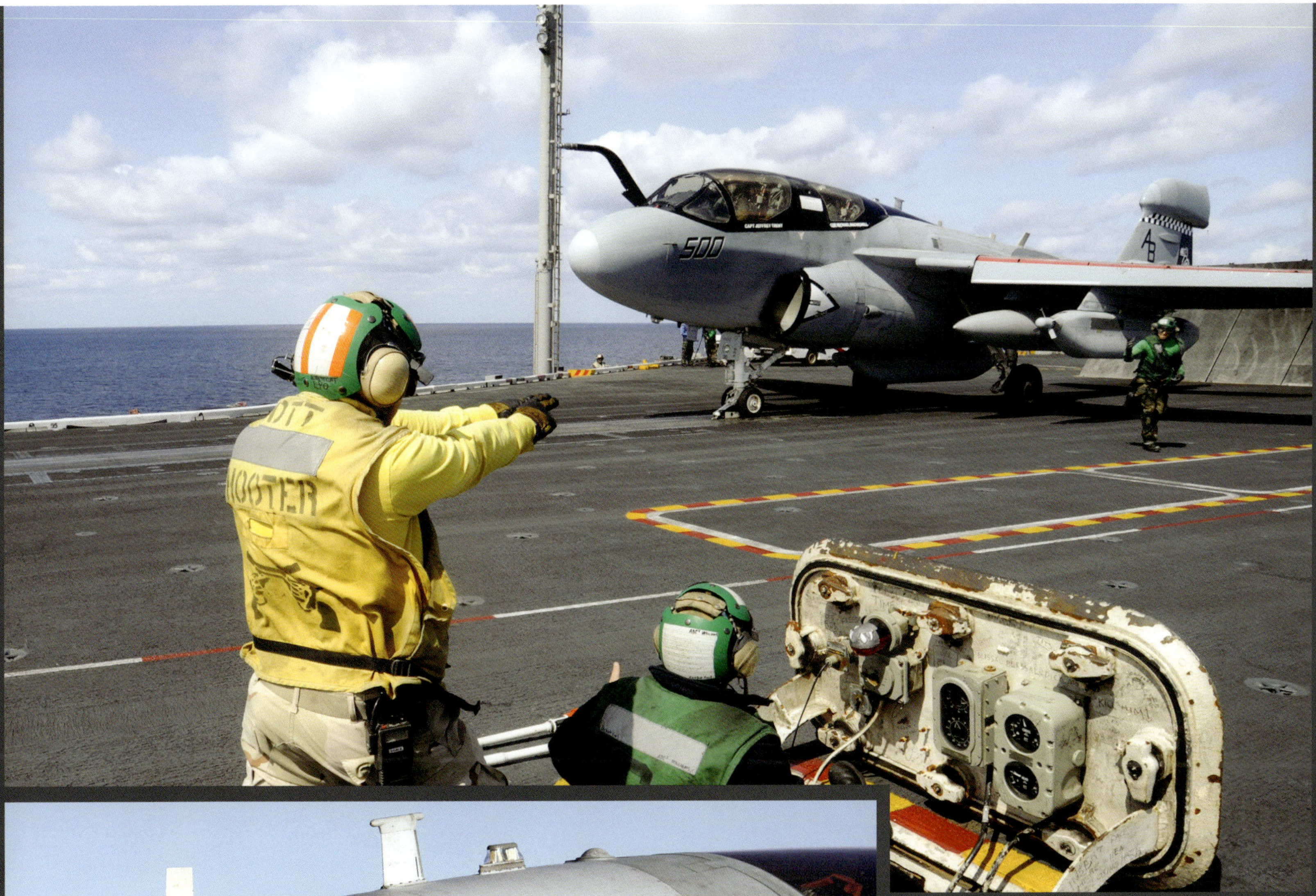

Photo:US Navy

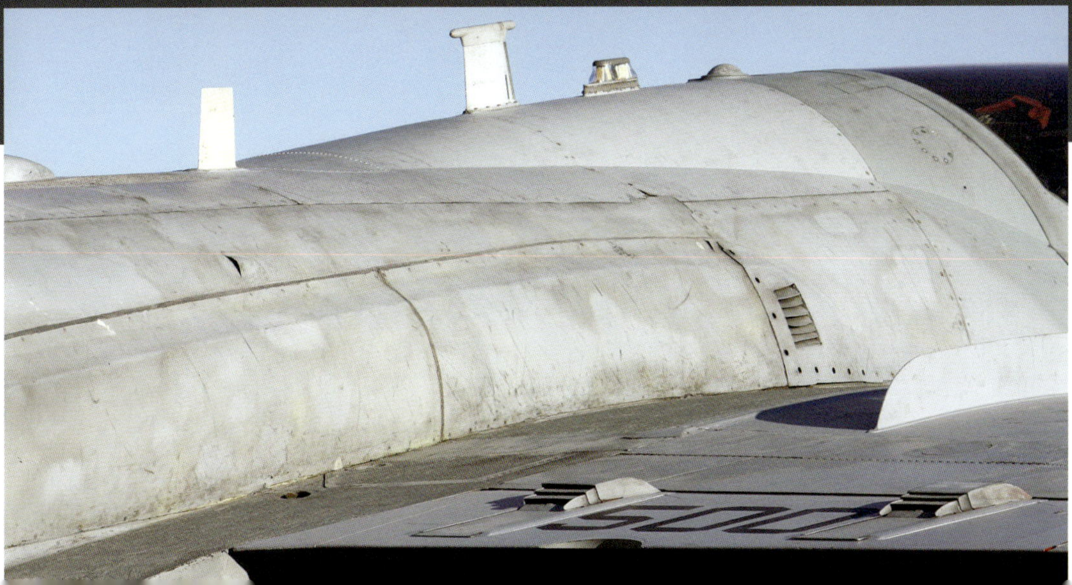

Photo:Akira Watanabe

Above: The Shooter is signaling to the pilot of a Prowler, hooked up for a launch from the starboard bow catapult, while a green shirt is running for cover, after having checked the jet a final time. The blast doors behind the aircraft are up, making sure that deck crew and equipment isn't blown away during launch. Left: The starboard fuselage, seen from behind the wing. Notice the fuselage fairing.

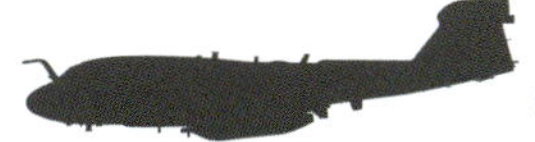

The Prowler's Wings

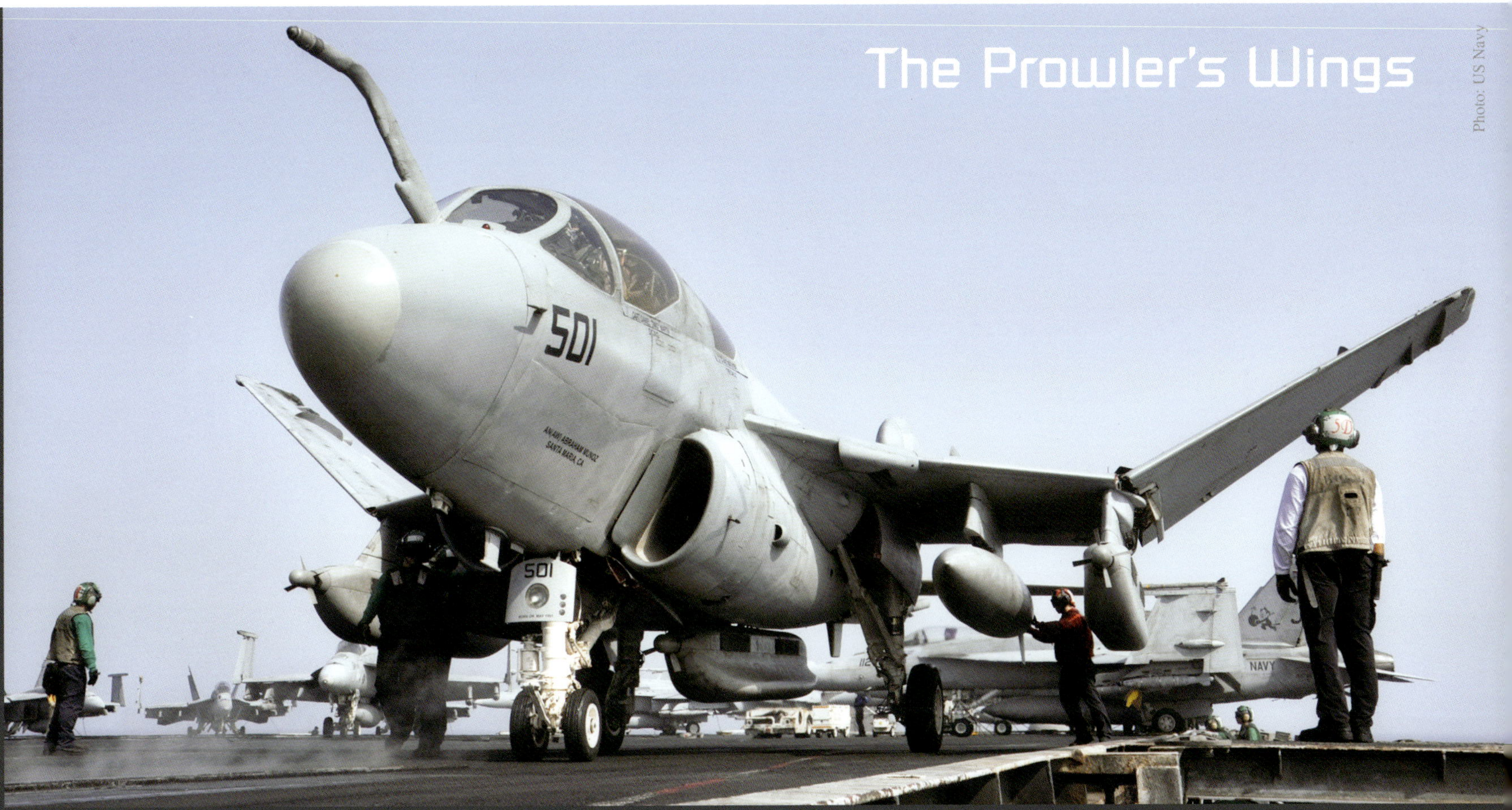

Photo: US Navy

Photo: David Draycott

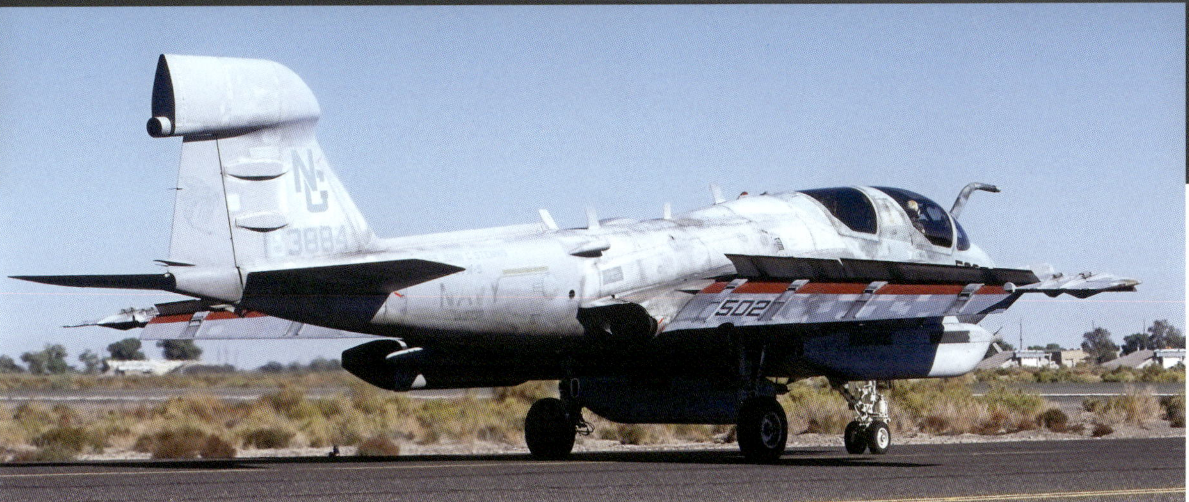

Above: A Prowler is taking position on the ship's bow to be lauched off cat 4 and the folded wings are brought down. Notice the large number of Super Hornets in the back, loaded with smart bombs.

The EA-6B Prowler has a wingspan of 16 meter. The wings are quite complex on the Prowler; not only because of the folding mechanism, but also because of the speed brakes, leading edge slats, trailing edge flaps and large spoilers, seen deployed in the photo to the left.

Above: The wing tip of the folded starboard wing, with the formation strips, navigation lights and speed brake actuators. Look at the static discharger on the trailing edge of it.

Left: This very cool photo shows a Prowler landing at El Centro after a training mission. It gives a good idea how wide the wings of the aircraft actually are. Look at the completely lowered leading edge slats and trailing edge flaps. This aircraft is the CAG of VAQ-129, "Vikings" which is a unit that at the time of writing celebrates its 60th anniversary. In the early days of the Vikings, the unit was a Heavy Attack Squadron flying the A-3 Skywarrior and saw a lot of action in the Vietnam War. In the 1970s the unit transferred to the EA-6B Prowler and would remain on the type for 35 years. Today, the unit is still operational and flies the supersonic EA-18G Growler.

Above: Only seconds after having caught the wire on the deck of the USS Nimitz, the wings of this Prowler, assigned to VAQ-142 "The Gray Wolves" are folded. Before doing so, the trailing edge flaps are brought up. Notice the wing fences ensuring the airflow over the wings. A Green Shirt signals that the arresting cable can be pulled back so that the next aircraft can land safely. Look at the large wing fences, making sure that the direction of the airflow is guaranteed.

Right: When the wings are folded, this red indicator can be seen on the lower wing, near the folding mechanism. A detail often overlooked.

The Ram Air Turbine, located on top of the port wing root. In case of loss of power, the turbine is deployed, which provides emergency power to the jet's systems.

Photo: Dave Chng

Photo: Dave Chng

Photo: Akira Watanabe

Photo: Philip Stevens

Above: A Prowler is fixed to the deck with multiple chains at the many tie-down points. The folded wings are supported by struts. The photos to the right shows where these struts are fixed in the wing and fuselage.

Photo: Dave Chng

Photo: Dave Chng

Photo: Akira Watanabe

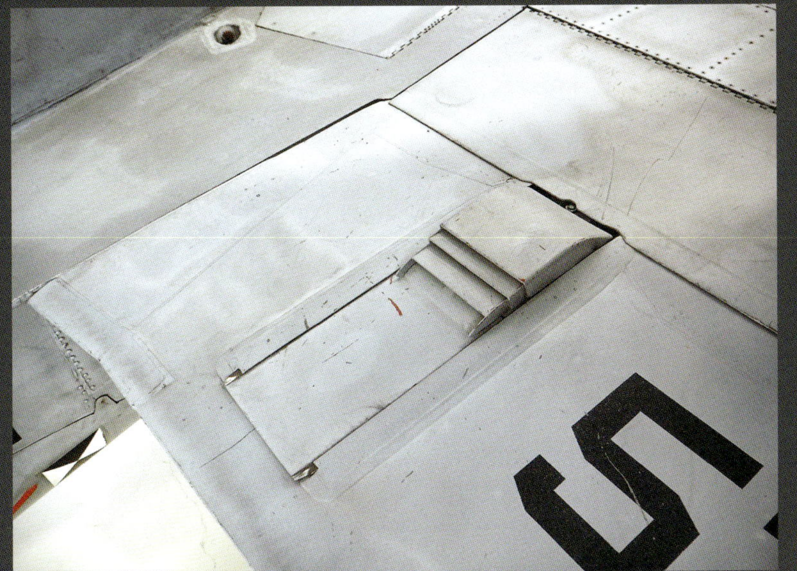

US Navy jets need to be able to fly at low speeds during approach; landing on the crowded deck of an aircraft carrier is hard enough, let alone if you have to do it at a high landing speed. This is why the Prowler, as so many Navy aircraft, is equipped with systems to provide stability during slow apporaches, such as large trailing edge flaps and long leading edge slats. The photo on the opposite page shows the position of the slats in folded position. The slats can be lowered to 27,5 degrees and are operated by means of 4 actuators per wing.

The trailing edge flaps are also operated by means of 4 actuators - actually, two for each flap - with one of them seen in the up-position in the photo to the left. During landing and take off, the flaps are lowered 20 degrees. Notice how a cut-out is made in the inner flap, providing room for the drop tank. Look at the structure of the underside of the wing and the reinforcements on it.

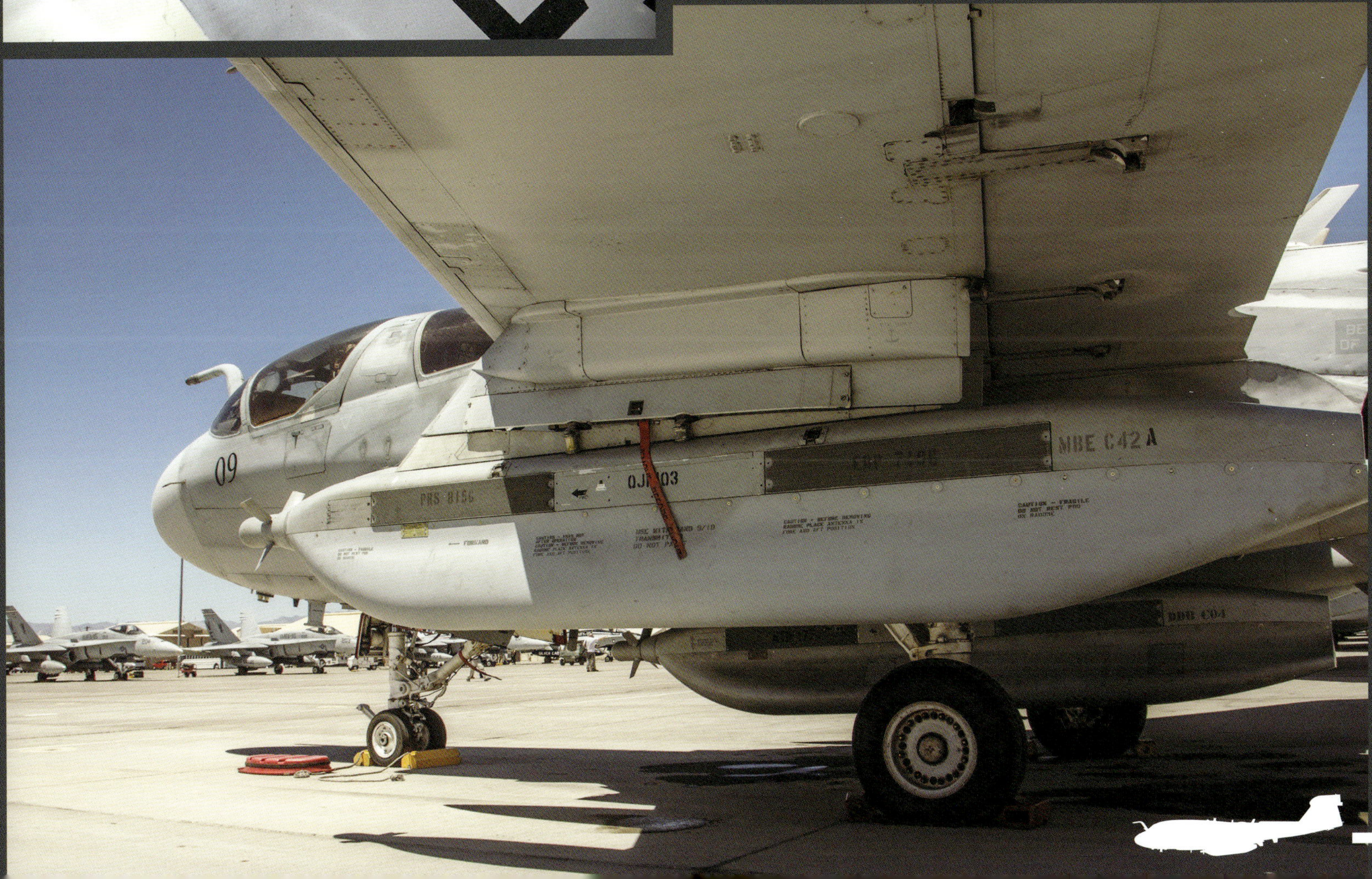

Photo: Dave Ching

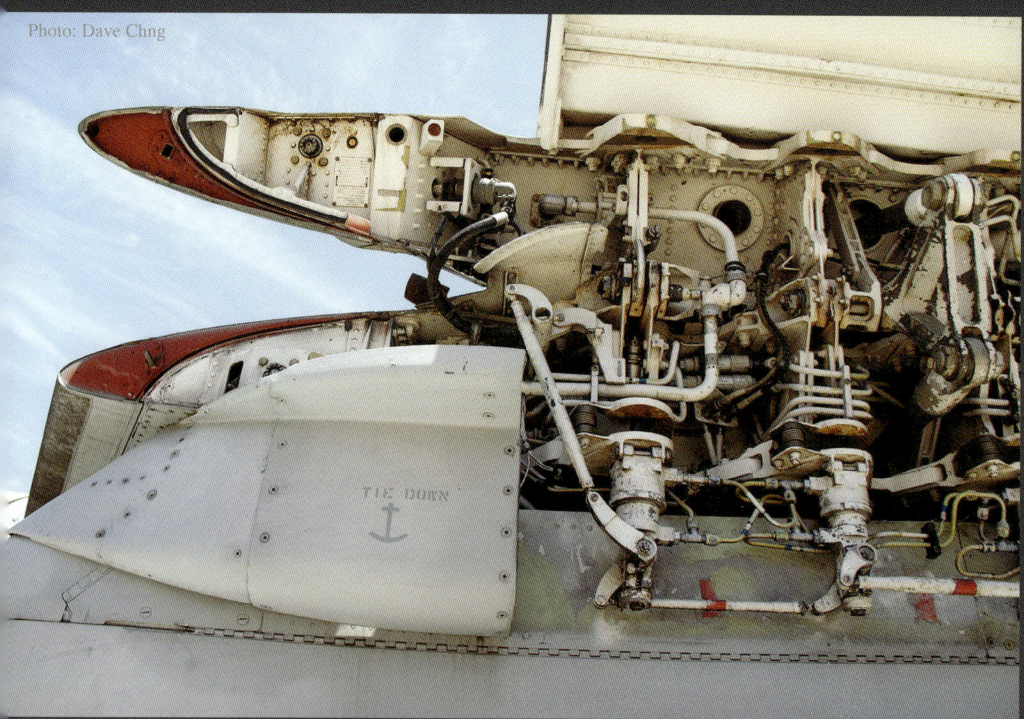

Photo: Dave Chng

Photo: Dave Chng

Time to get a good close-up look at the wing folding mechanism of the EA-6B Prowler. Folding the wings brings the span of the Prowler from 16 meters back to just 7,6 meters, meaning that two aircraft can be parked on the spot of just one with wings unfolded. As said before: space is very precious on the deck of an aircraft carrier.

The first thing to know is that both the leading edge slats and trailing edge flaps are always flush with the wings when they are folded. Roughly halfway through the wings, the folding mechanism is located. There are 4 major attachment points connecting the outer wing with the inner wing and a single large actuator in the middle of the mechanism. Look at the position of the flaps in the photo to the right.

Photo: Dave Chng

Grumman EA-6B Prowler
Wings
Photo: Dave Chng
Photo: Dave Chng
Photo: Dave Chng

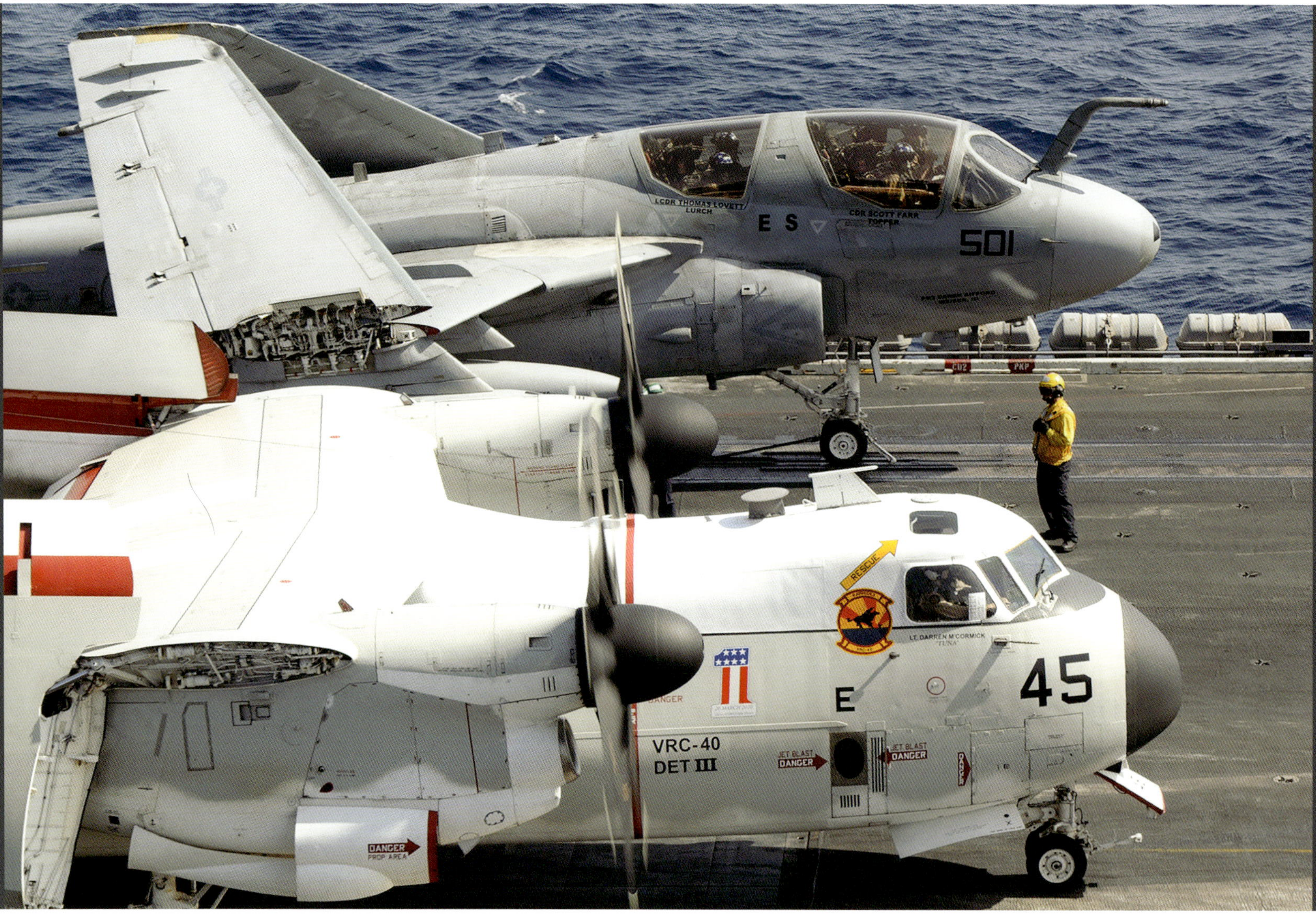

Photo: US Navy

Above: This photo shows an EA-6B Prowler fixed to the catapult on the deck of the aircraft carrier, still with the wings folded. It is waiting for a C2A Greyhound to pass. Look the different wing folding mechanisms - the Greyhound's wings fold backwards, while those of the Prowler fold upwards. The moment the COD has been launched, the Prowler will lower the wings and be launched from the ship.

Right: The trailing edge flap and aileron align with the wing when the wings are folded. Look at the grey wires and hydraulic lines in this area.

Photo: Dave Chng

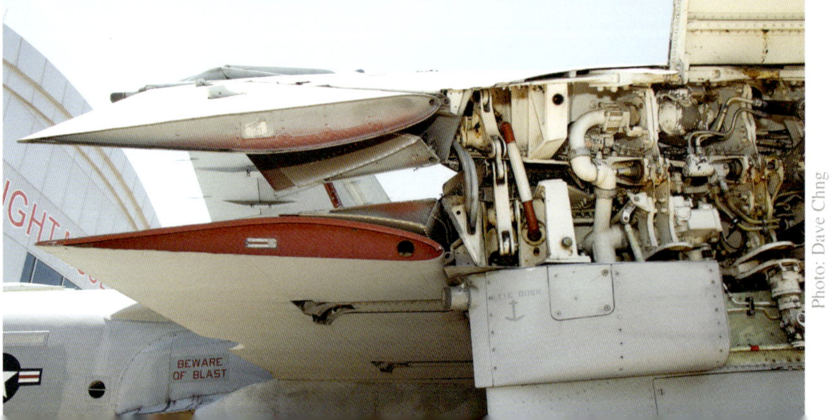

These photos show the folding mechanism of the starboard wing. Notice that the leading edge slats are pulled flush to the wing parts when they are folded. Over the folding mechanism, a rectangular door is located, that folds down flush with the upper part of the wing pylon. The photos show the four hinges, with in the centre the folding actuator. Notice that in front and aft of the mechanism, a tie down point is located. The photo above shows the lowered spoiler on the folded wingtip.

The locating of the speed brakes is reminiscent of the initial design of the Grumman Intruder. It being a dive bomber, the location of the speed brakes near the wing tips gave it a more accurate drag control than when they were installed on the aft fuselage. The position was kept for the EA-6B Prowler. Notice the large ECM antenna located inboard of the speed brake in the photo to the right.

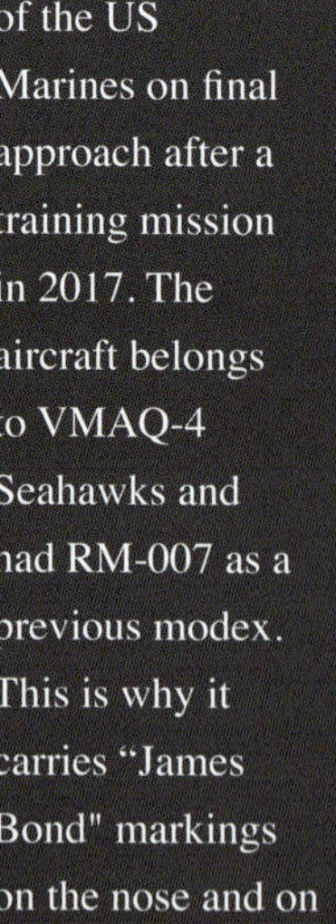

Left: A Prowler of the US Marines on final approach after a training mission in 2017. The aircraft belongs to VMAQ-4 Seahawks and had RM-007 as a previous modex. This is why it carries "James Bond" markings on the nose and on the insides of the speed brakes.

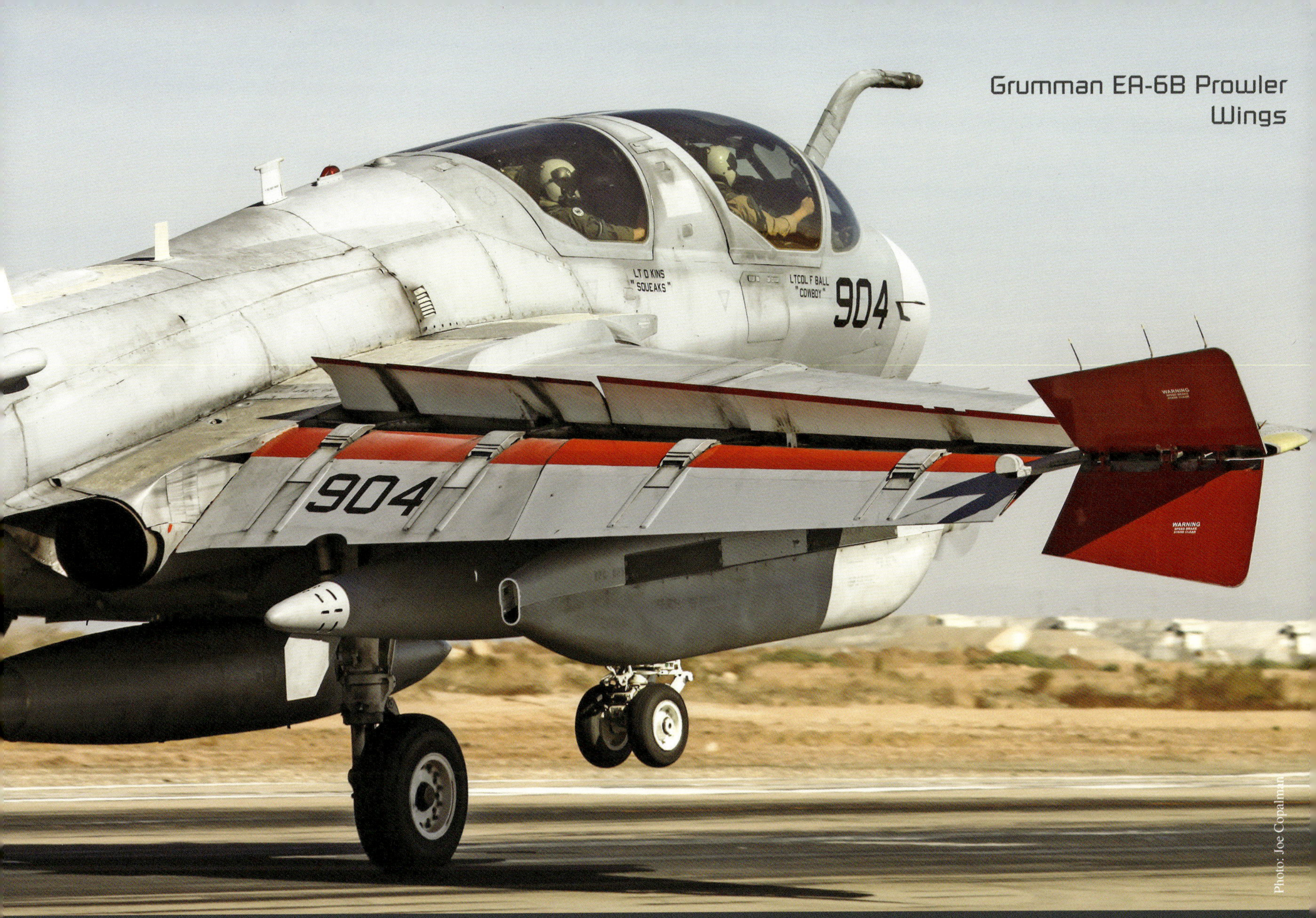

Photo: Joe Copalman

Above: An EA-6B from VAQ-129 conducts Field Carrier Landing practice at NAF El Centro in southern California in November 2010. Though based at NAS Whidbey Island in Washington State, VAQ-129 regularly sent training detachments to El Centro to take advantage of the year-round favorable weather conditions. Look at the detail of the speed brake, the spoilers and the trailing edge flaps. Notice the shape of the flap where the droptank is located. Three static dischargers are fixed to the upper speed brake.

Photo: Akira Watanabe

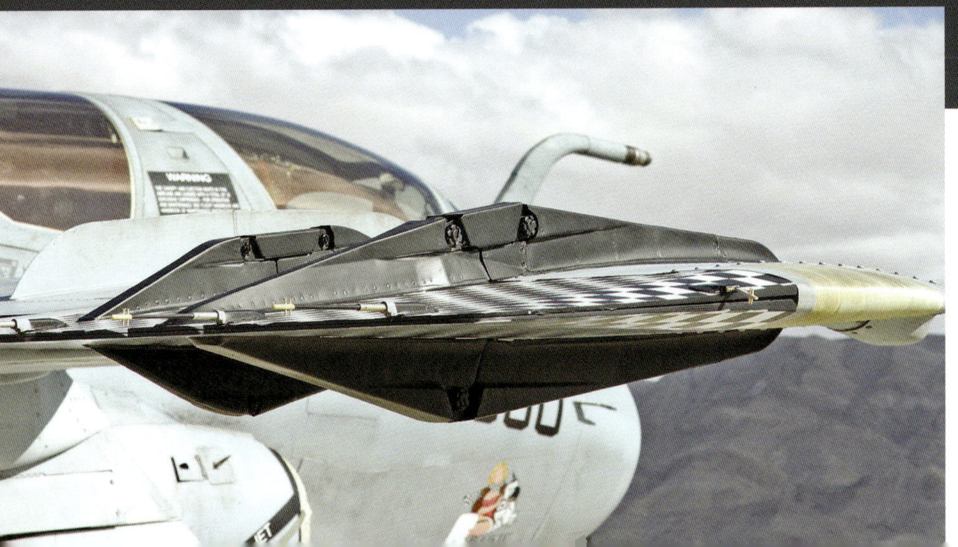

Left: The closed speed brakes of the starboard wing, showing the structure of the actuators.

Photo: Akira Watanabe

Flyin' the Prowler

The cockpits of the Prowler is where everything happens, so logically, we have an extensive chapter on it. The front cockpit is where the pilot sits; more specifically in the left seat. He or she is the only one with flight controls, as can be seen in the photo above. In the right seat sits the first of the Electronics Countermeasures Operators. This officer is responsable for navigation and communication jamming. The crew in the back have the task of jamming radars and other operating systems. During the different upgrades, the cockpits of the Prowler got modernised; logic, since there is nearly 50 years between the first version and the final ICAP-III version. The photo above shows the cockpit of an ICAP-I Prowler that was upgraded to an ICAP-II standard. Notice the AN/USQ-113 Communications jammer in front of the ECMO has been removed. Below it is the Direct View Radar Indicator with a cover, keeping out the light. Later versions have a better screen that doesn't necessitate the cover - see page 59. Look at the colour of the ejection seat covers.

Left: Rear Adm. J.R. Haley, the commander of Task Force 70 and Carrier Strike Group 5, closes the foldable step next to him prior to conducting a flight operation with the Gauntlets -VAQ-136 aboard the USS George Washington. The unit transferred not long after this photo was taken from the EA-6B Prowler to the EA-18G Growler.

Below left: The stick of the Prowler. It is filled with controls, such as a trim button, weapons release or the nose wheel steering.

Photo: MSC2 William Pittman, US Navy

Photo: Dave Cling

Photo: Dave Clng

A closer look at the pilot's station of a modernised Prowler of the US Marines. Compare it to the photo on page 56: this Prowler has the round Radar Display Indicator replaced by a large screen. Above it are two black screens: the Electronic Attitude Director Indicator - top - and the Electronic Horizontal Situation Indicator - below. To the right of the screens are some analogue instruments, such as an artificial horizon, a jaw rate indicator and a series of warning lights.

Above: The pilot's station, seen from the right hand seat. Look at the controle stick and the three screens in front of it. Fixed to the windscreen framing, is a handhold used mainly during launch from the deck. The Martin-Baker GRUEA-7 ejection seat is positioned quite close to the instrument panel. To the left of the pilot is the throttle, which can be seen in detail on the opposite page. Behind it are the light switches.

Photo: Dave Chng

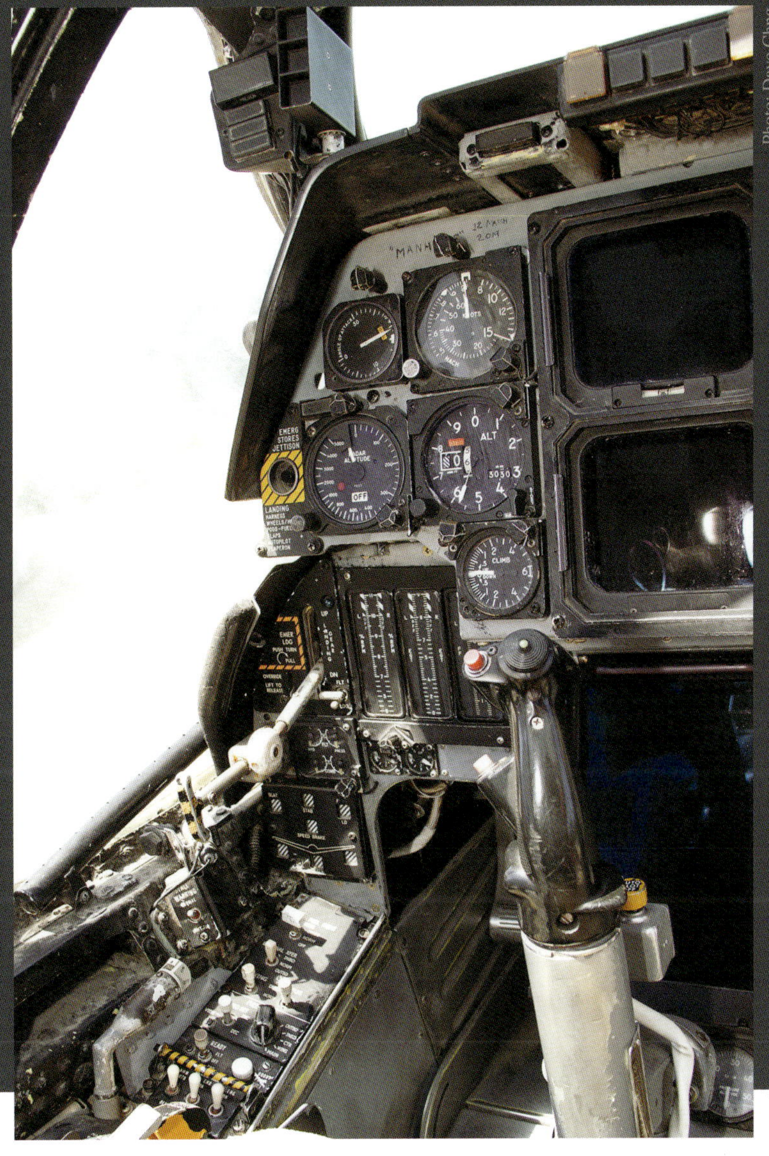

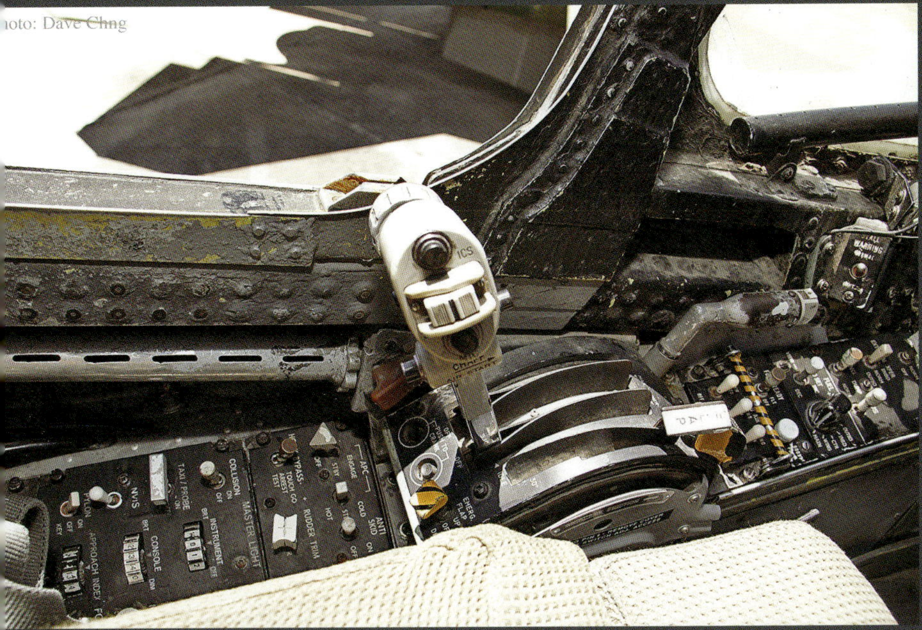

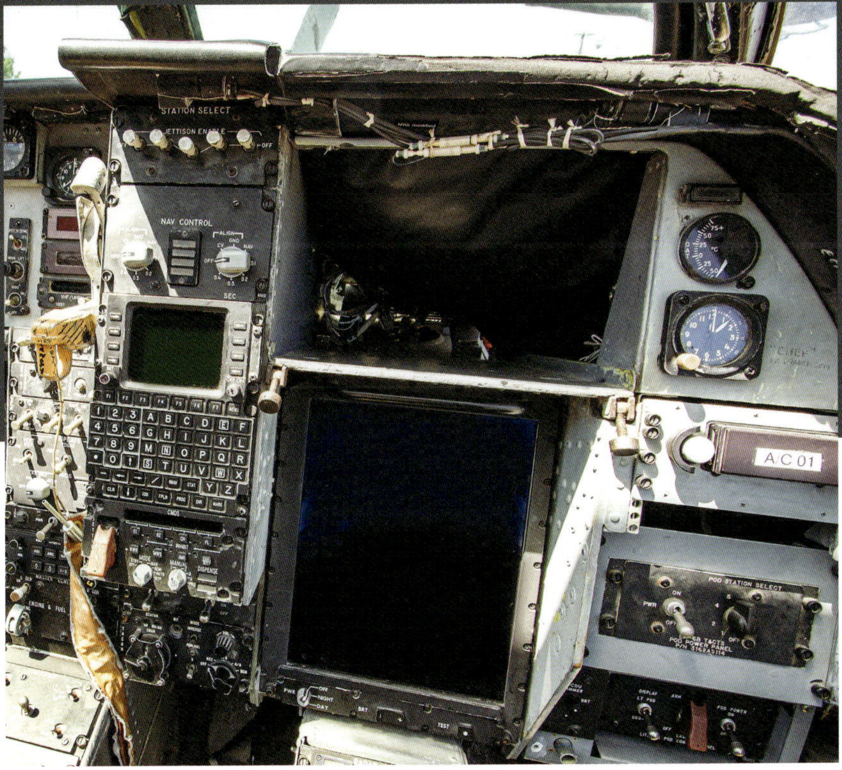

Photo: Dave Chng

Photo: Dave Chng

Above: A close-up of the analogue instruments to the left of the three screens. You can see the indicators for the Airspeed, Angle of Attack, Altitude, Rate of Climb and Radar Altitude. The grey handle to the left is to retract or lower the landing gear, while the vertical bars next to it offer information on the engines, such as RPM, exhaust temperature or fuel flow.
Left: The right hand station with a large screen in stead of the older type and covered Direct View Radar Indicator.

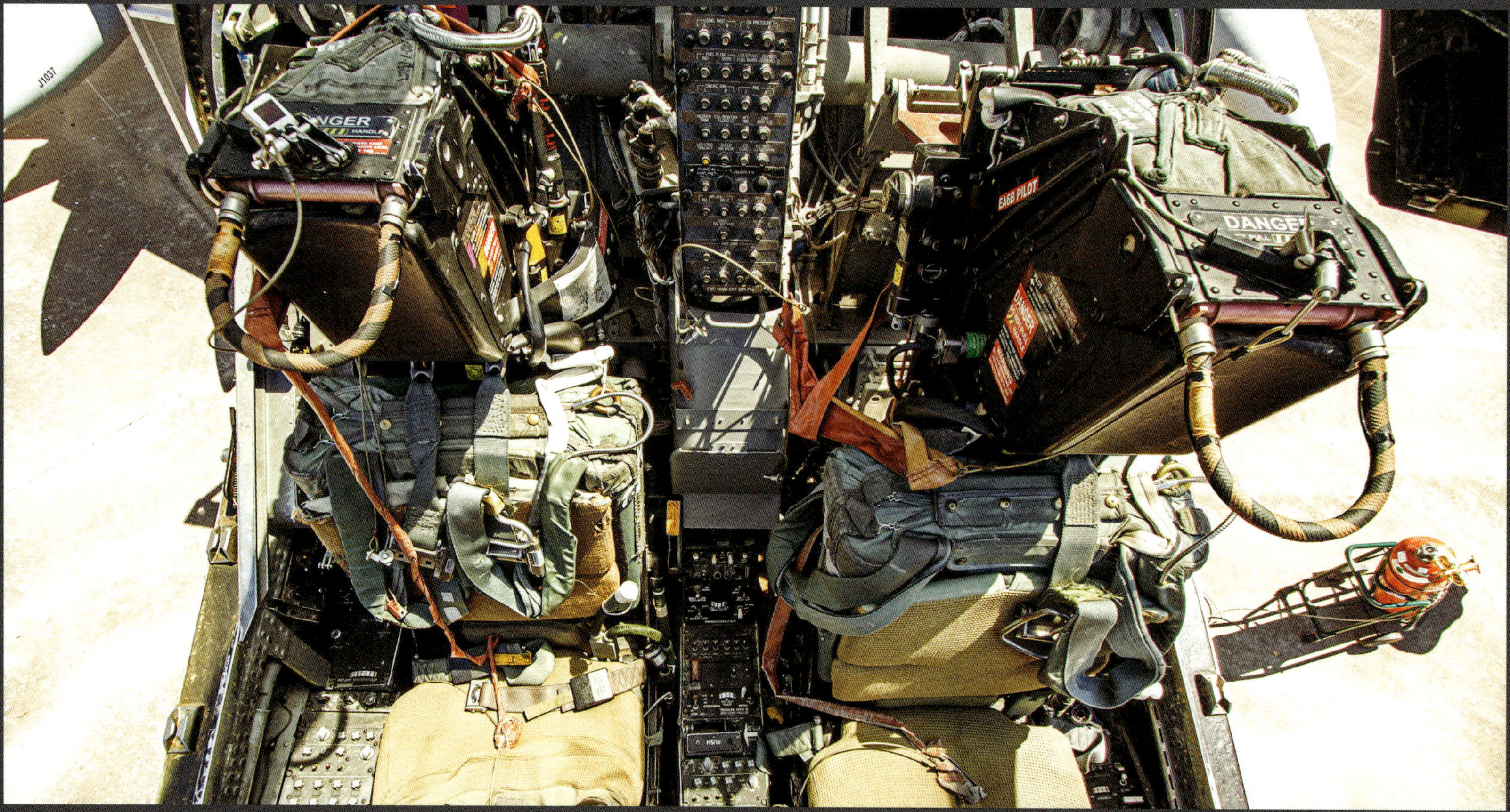

Above: Looking down into the front cockpit, this is what you see. Notice the large number of circuit brakers located in between the two seats. The pilot's seat, in this view on the right is positioned slighty forward of the ECMO's.

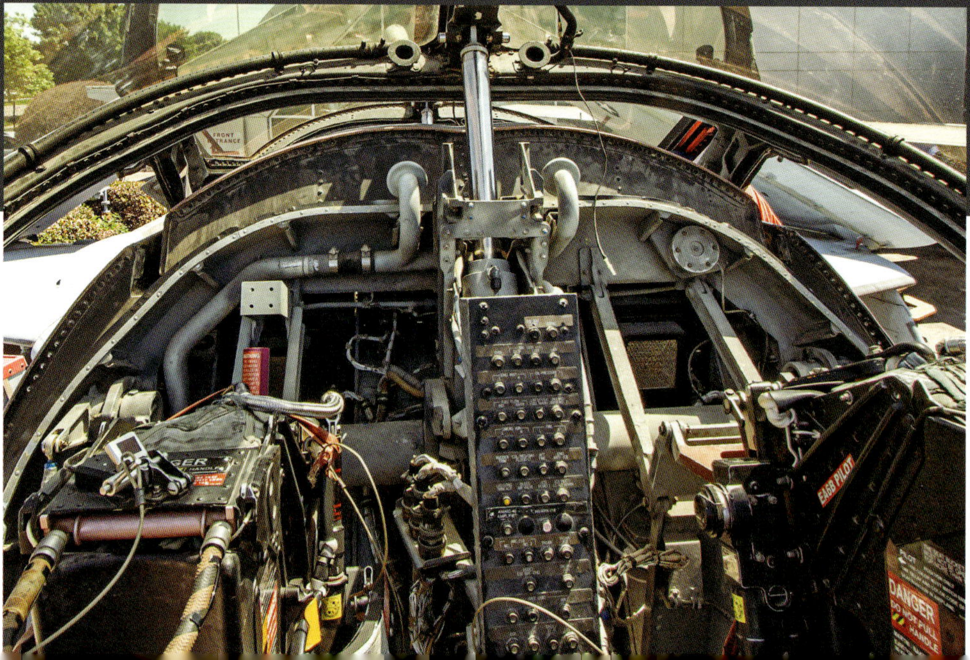

Right: The same area as in the photo above, but a little higher. This is the area behind the two forward ejection seats. The large canopy is lowered and raised by means of a single hydraulically operated actuator, located behind the circuit breaker panel. Look at all the wiring and air conditioning piping running in this area. Notice the two hinges of the forward canopy. The outer parts of the cockpit are black, the interior itself is painted grey.

Grumman EA-6B Prowler Cockpit

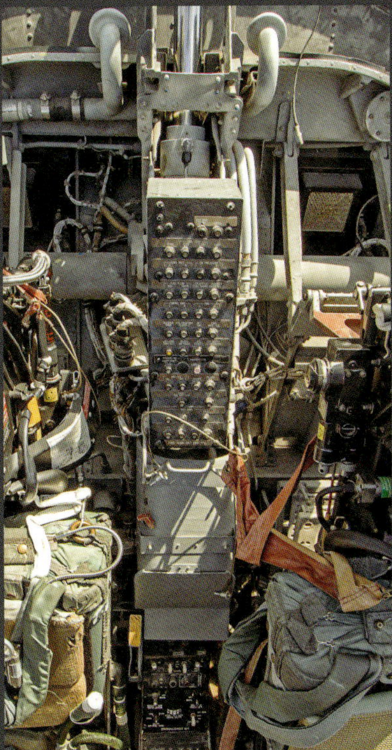

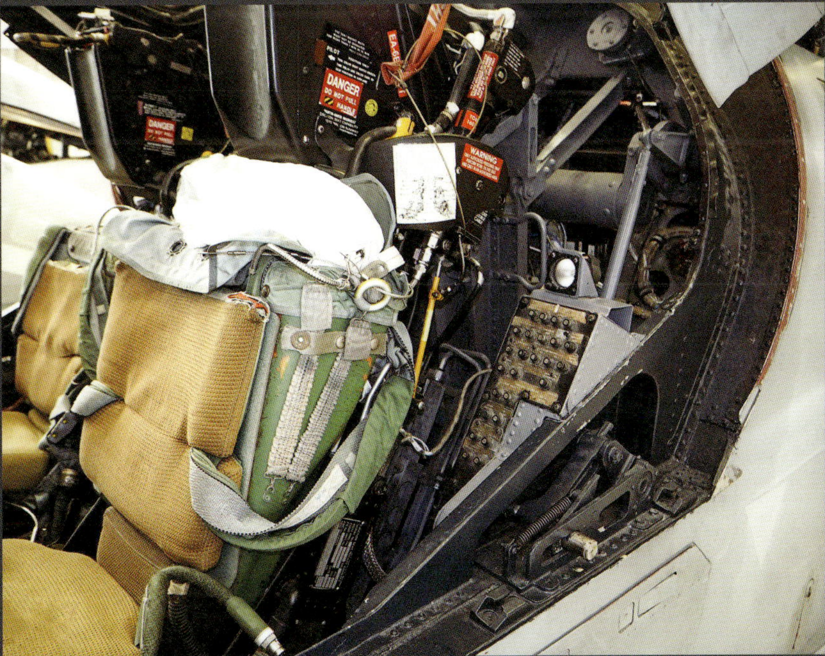

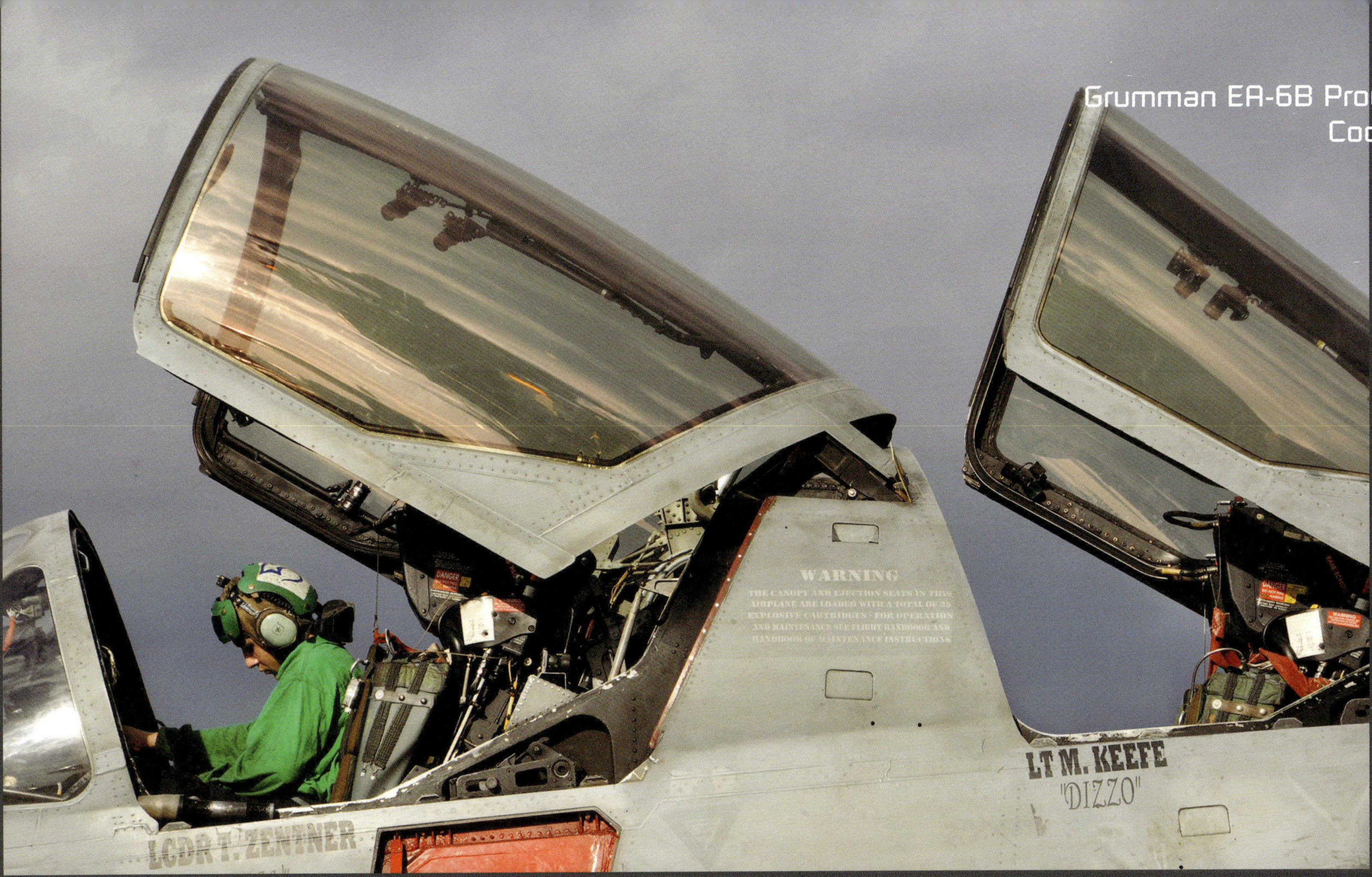

Photo: US Navy

Photo: Dave Cling

Photo: Akira Watanabe

Above: This great overall view of the cockpits of the Prowler reveales a lot of interesting details, not in the least the cockpit and canopy framing, which is painted black.

Left: The area behind the pilot's seat in detail. Notice another panel of circuit breakers and a cockpit light. Notice the locking system on the cockpit framing, and the wiring connected to the ejection seat. These seats are very much like those used in the F-14 A and B models, but only have one overhead ejection handle and not two like in the Tomcat.

The ejection seats in the Prowler are Martin-Baker GRUEA-7s, which are based on the Mk.7. These have a proven track record and were used in many fast jets, such as the Tomcat, Intruder and Prowler, but also the F-8 Crusader. Ejection is possible by pulling the overhead handle or the lower handle, situated in between the pilots legs.

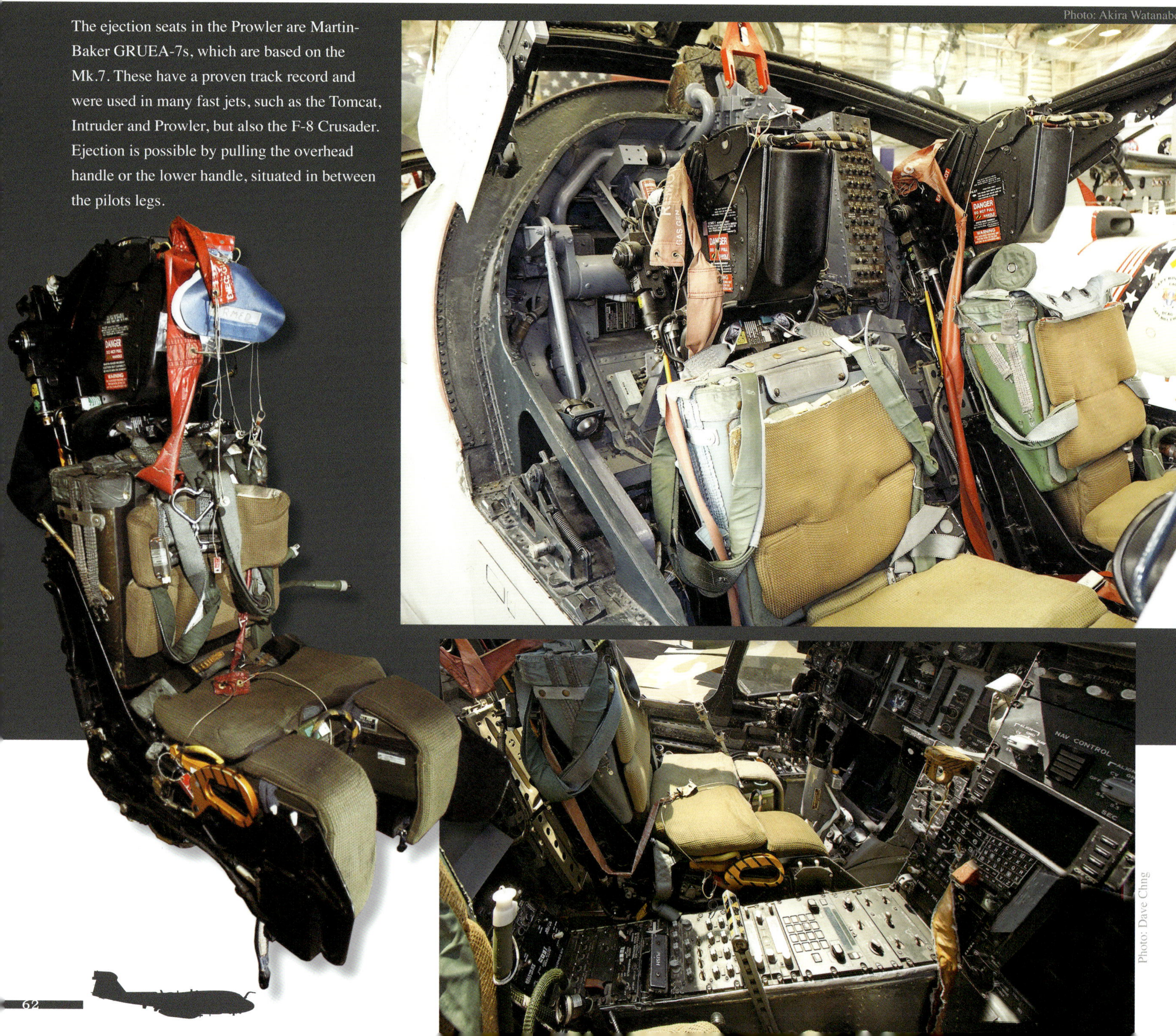

Photo: Akira Watanabe

Photo: Dave Cring

Photo: Dave Ching

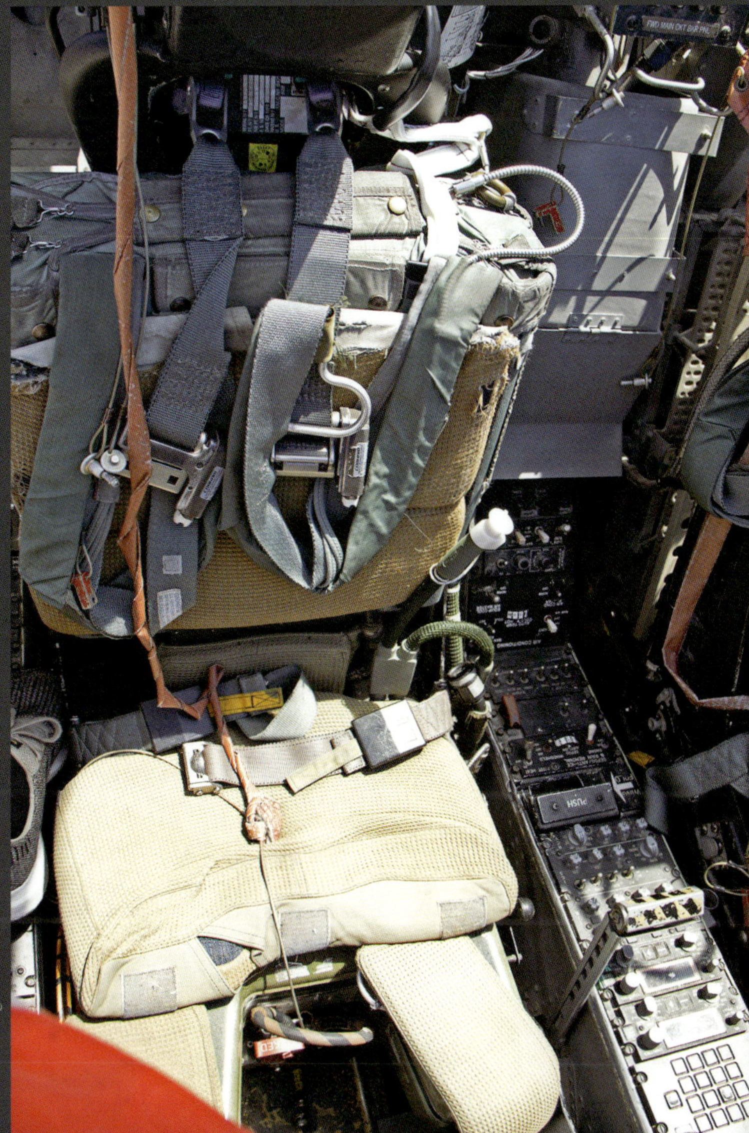

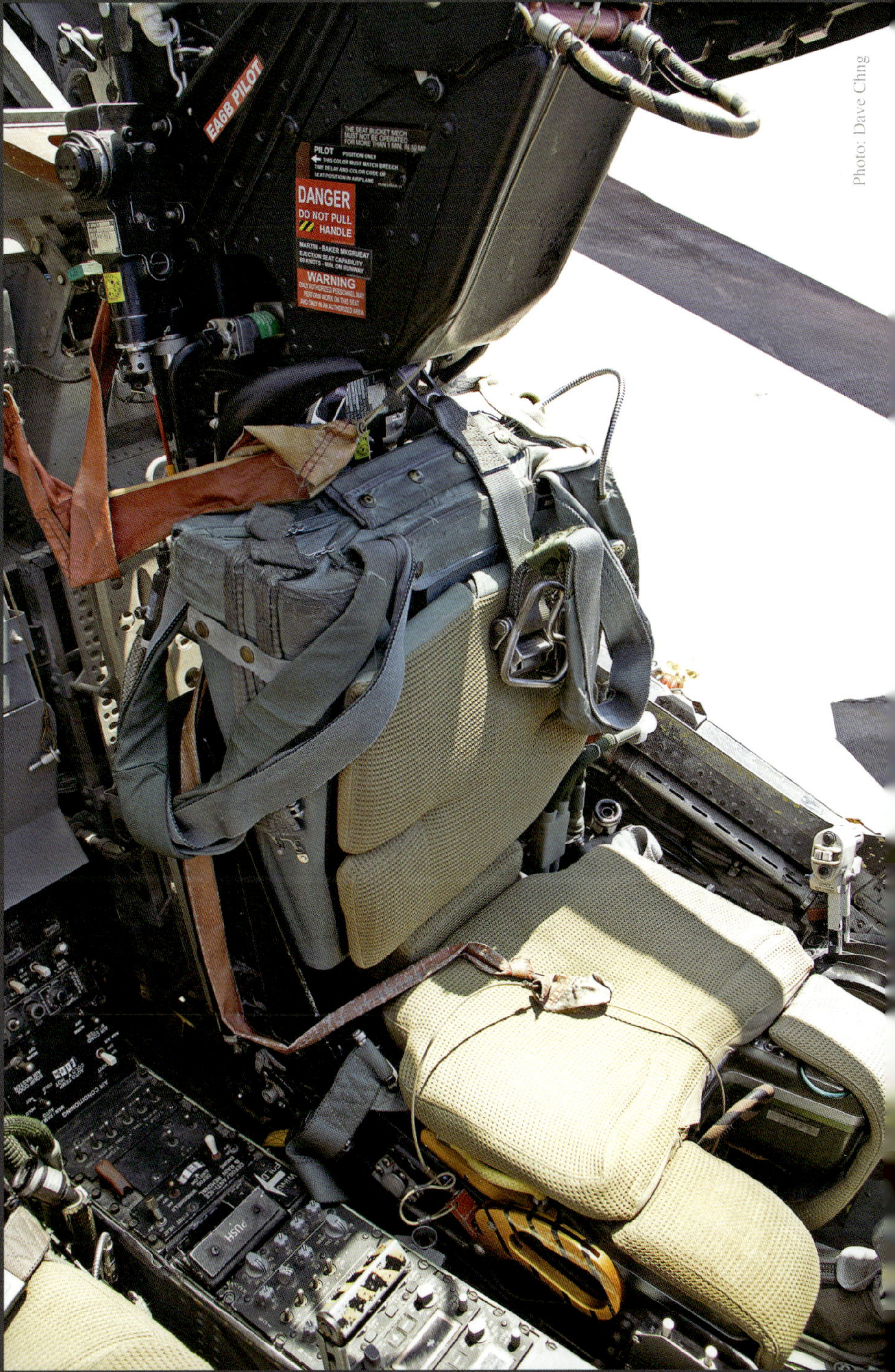

Photo: Dave Ching

These photos show the forward ejection seats in detail. All 4 seats in the EA-6B are the same. Behind the light brown seating is the green fiberglass parachute container, the harness are light grey. The yellow-and-black handle to the right side of the seat is the Emergency Restraint Release Handle. To the left is the connection for the G-suit. Underneath the lower seating, the emergency oxygen is located. Here, a survival kit is stowed as well. Notice the large black wing-fold handle located on the central instrument console.

Aft cockpit

The aft cockpit holds the workstations for two Electronic Countermeasures Operators - ECMO - each with a large screen immediately in front of them. These crew members have no view forward, only to the side. Below the video screen, the Digital Display Indicator Control panel is located. Notice the handhold in the middle of the forward instrument panel. Four analogue instruments in the middle of the latter, give the ECMOs an idea of the position of the aircraft.

Right: The aft cockpit, this time seen from the starboard side of the aircraft. The Electronic Countermeasures Operators make sure that radar systems are jammed and tracked, in case they need to be destroyed with an AGM-88 HARM missile.

Below right: A close-up of the central part of the forward instrument panel. Notice the Artificial Horizon, Altimeter, Pressure Altitude indicator and Airspeed indicator. Above it is the main circuit breaker control panel

Below: A head-on view of the forward instrument panel. Look at the shape of the cockpit framing.

Photo: Dave Chng

Photo: Akira Watanabe

Photo: Dave Chng

Right: A look inside the aft cockpit from the port side of the aircraft. Look at the details of the cockpit side walls with the padding and the structure of the panels. In between the seats, the Tactical Jamming System control panel is located. Below it, UHF and VHF radio control panels can be found. The jamming pods, which are operated from the aft cockpit, can generate signals within seven frequency bands. Thanks to the TACAN data link, introduced with the ICAP II upgrade, two EA-6Bs can fly together during coordinated electronic warfare missions.

Above & left: The two Martin-Baker GRUEA-7 ejection seats in the aft cockpit. Notice the framing around the seats and the many electrical wires running aft of them.

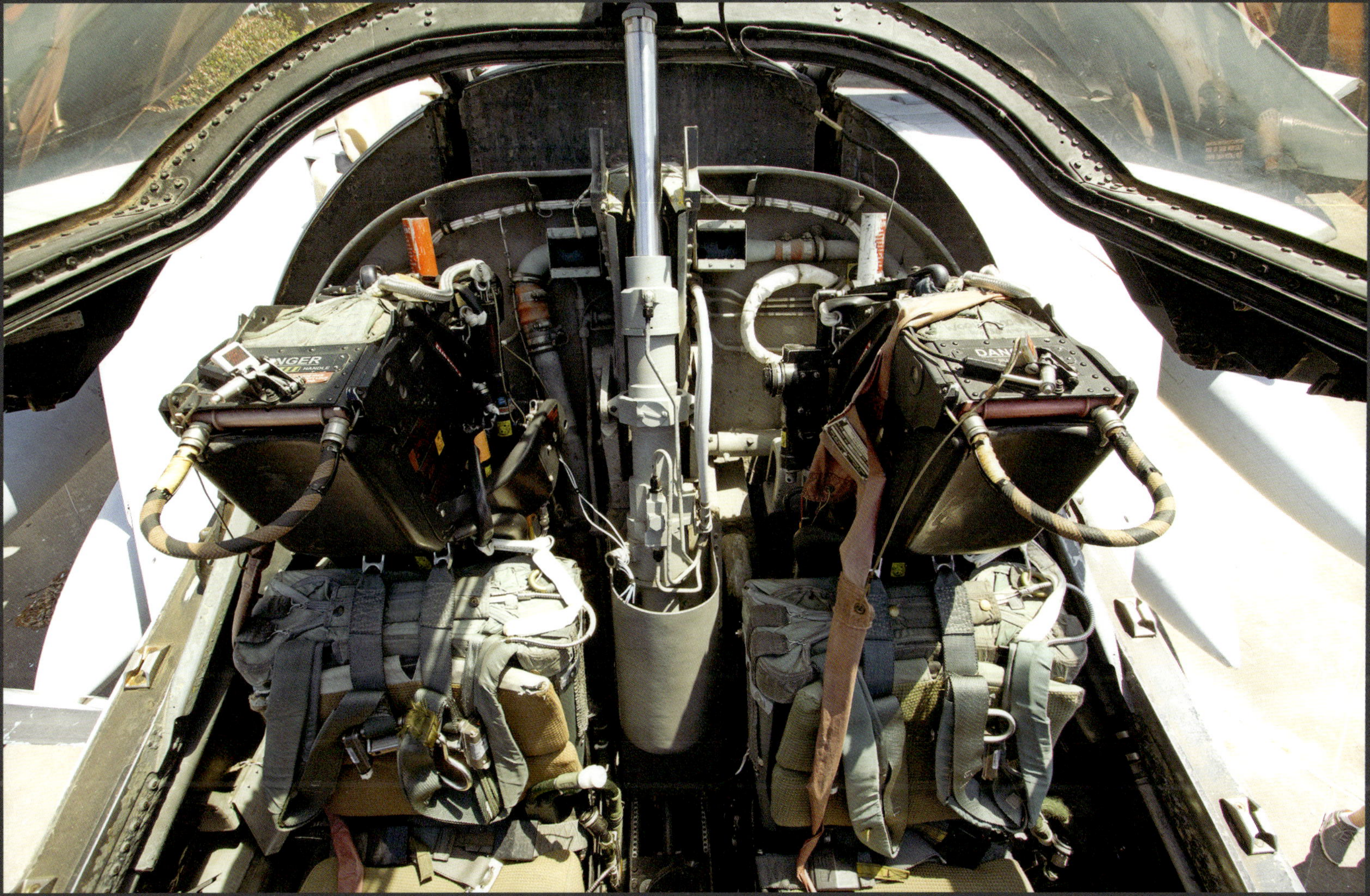

Photo: Dave Chng

Above: This photo shows the area in between the two ejection seats with the hydraulically operated canopy actuator prominent. Notice how the air conditioning piping runs differently compared to the front cockpit. Look at the brackets located on the cockpit framing where the canopy connections fit when it is closed.

Right: The locking system on the aft cockpit framing is quite different from the forward one. Again, notice the bundles of electrical wiring on the inside of the protective structure.

Photo: Akira Watanabe

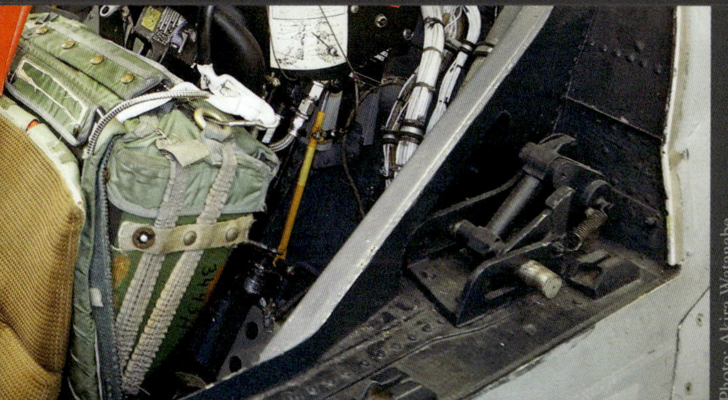

The photos on this page give a closer look at the canopy framing of the Prowler. On the central bar of each canopy, a pair of cockpit lights is located, enabling the crew to continue to work during nighttime missions.

Below: Both front and aft canopy have a pair of protective plates covering the hinges. This photo shows the aft canopy with the GPS antenna immediately behind it.

Photo: Stephan Ortmann

Above: An awesome photo of a Prowler dropping flares. On the outer wing pylon, it is carrying a HARM anti-radiation missile, used to destroy enemy radar systems. The weapons travels at nearly Mach 2 once fired and has a 66 kg warhead. Left: The crew of this Prowler are preparing for another mission. Notice the rear-view mirrors on the forward canopy framing.

Landing the Prowler

When an aircraft operates from an aircraft carrier, it'll better have a very strong landing gear. It's not landing, but rather smashing on the deck for these aircraft, which is why the Prowler is equipped with an extremely strong landing gear. In this chapter, we'll take a closer look at it. The photo above shows the Prowler's parts of the landing equipment - nose landing gear, main gear and arrestor hook - moments before it catches the wire on board of the USS Theodore Rossevelt. Looking at the photo, the radome of the aircraft is a replacement.

Right: The nose gear of the Prowler, seen from the port side, looking forward. The gear folds aft into the wheelbay by means of a support strut, connected low on the main strut.

Grumman EA-6B Prowler Front Landing Gear

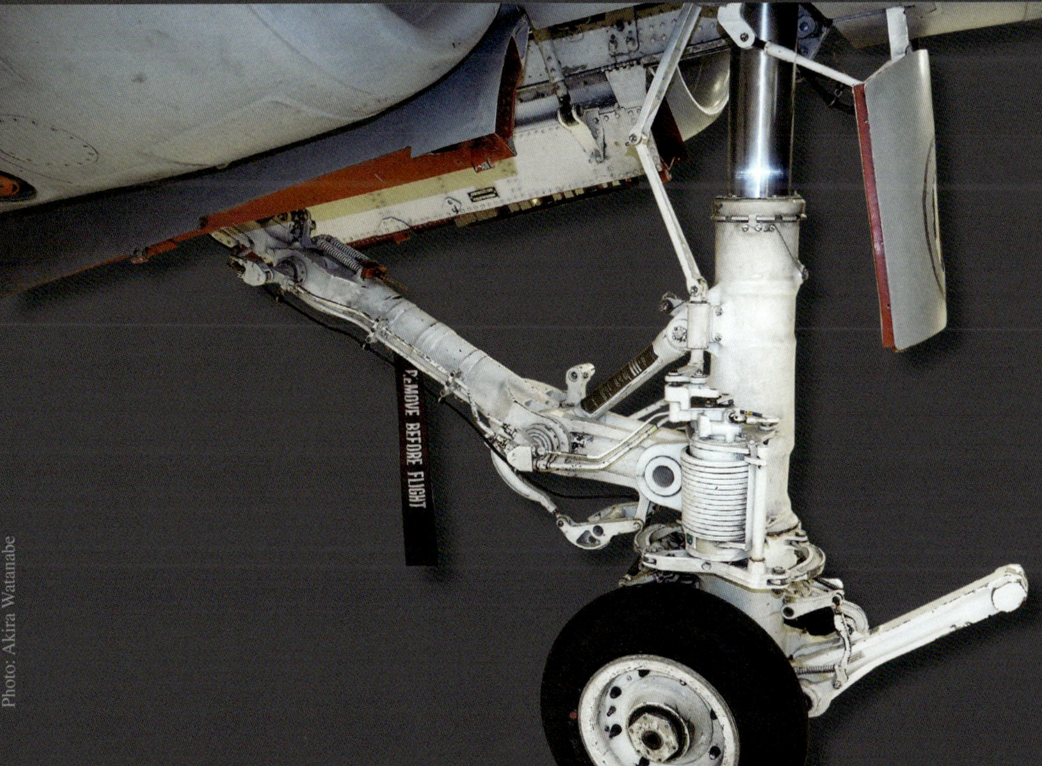

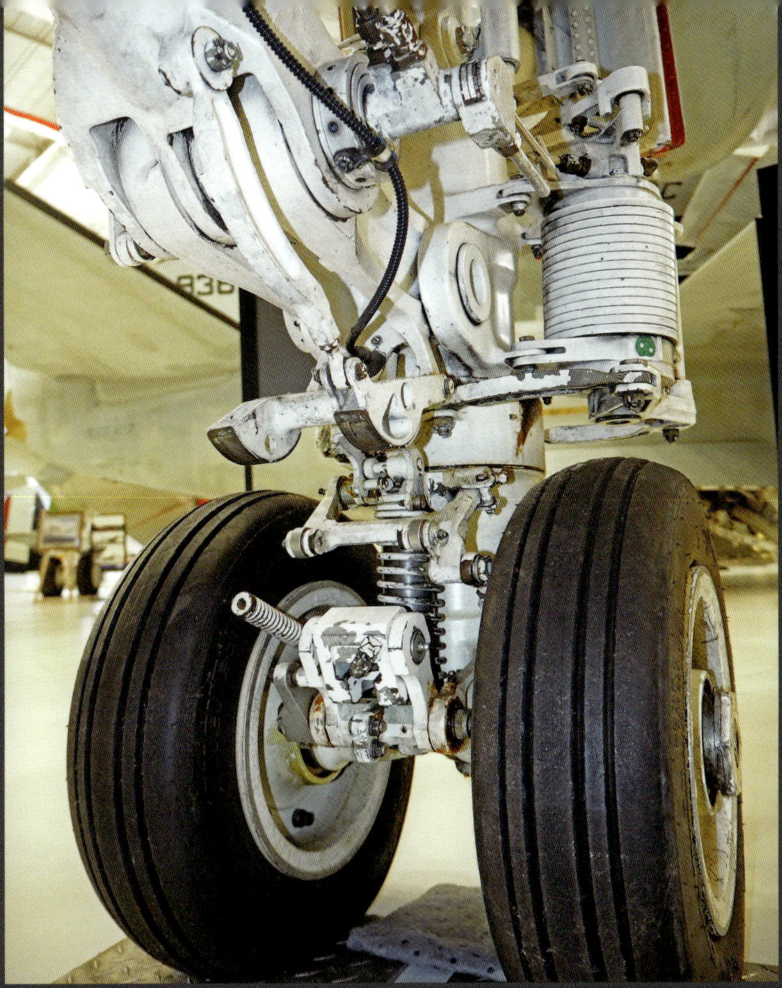

Photo: Akira Watanabe

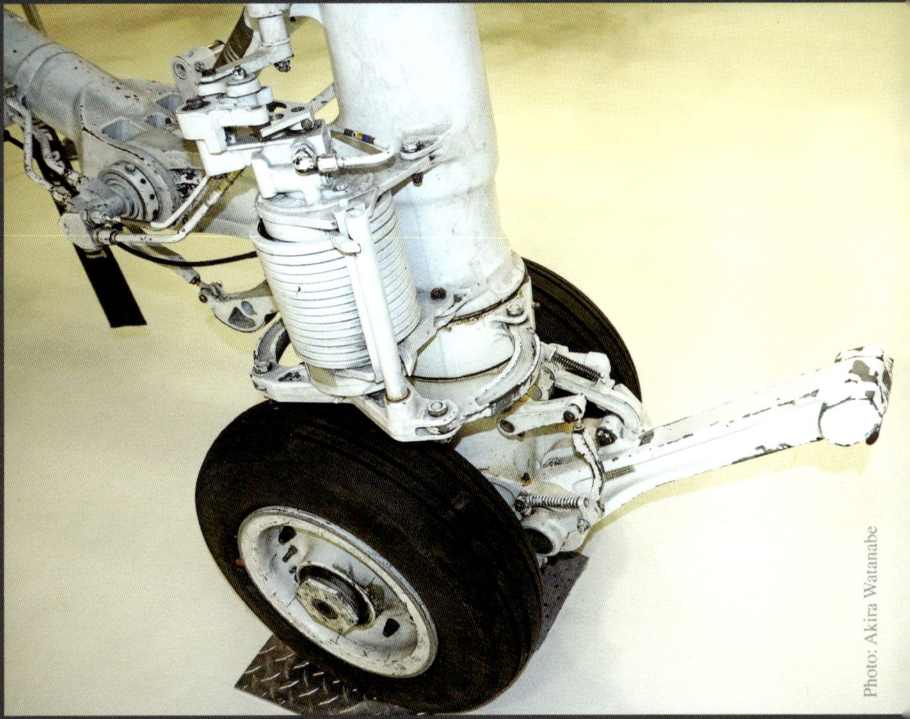

Photo: Akira Watanabe

Photo: Akira Watanabe

The nose gear is equipped with a launch bar to the front, which connect to the catapult shuttle. The gear has two 50,8 cm high wheels, each 14 cm wide. The system employs a strong air-oil shock strut, making sure that the aircraft can survive even the hardest of deck landings. The nose gear has a large shimmy damper on the starboard side. The pilot can steer the aircraft by turning the nose gear; for this a button has to be pressed, located on the control stick. This enables him to manoeuvre the jet around the always busy and crowded flight deck of the aircraft carrier. Aft of the gear, in between the wheels, the connection point for the holdback bar is located.

Notice the highly polished hydraulic cylinder in the photo to the left and the three forward gear doors.

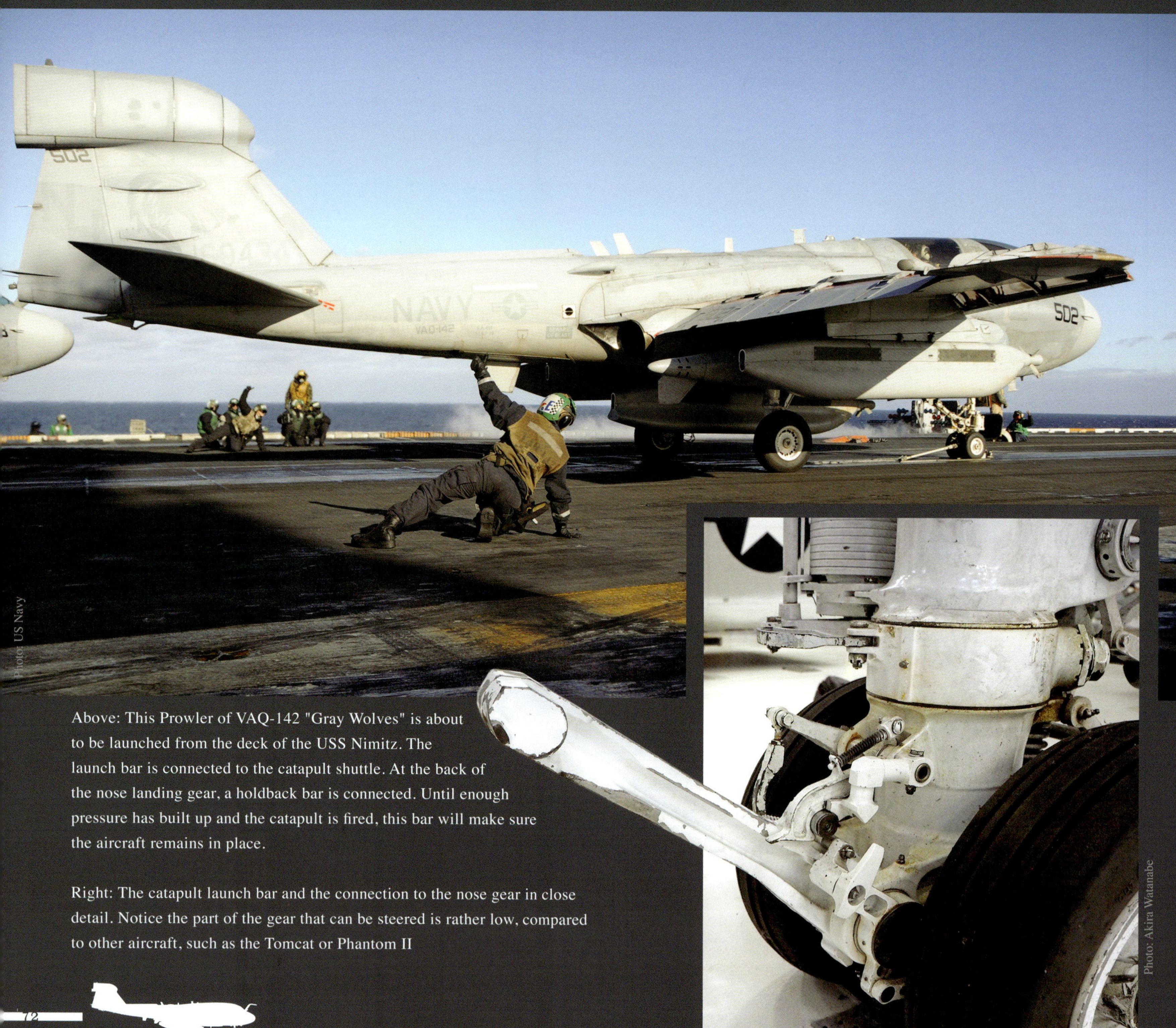

Above: This Prowler of VAQ-142 "Gray Wolves" is about
to be launched from the deck of the USS Nimitz. The
launch bar is connected to the catapult shuttle. At the back of
the nose landing gear, a holdback bar is connected. Until enough
pressure has built up and the catapult is fired, this bar will make sure
the aircraft remains in place.

Right: The catapult launch bar and the connection to the nose gear in close
detail. Notice the part of the gear that can be steered is rather low, compared
to other aircraft, such as the Tomcat or Phantom II

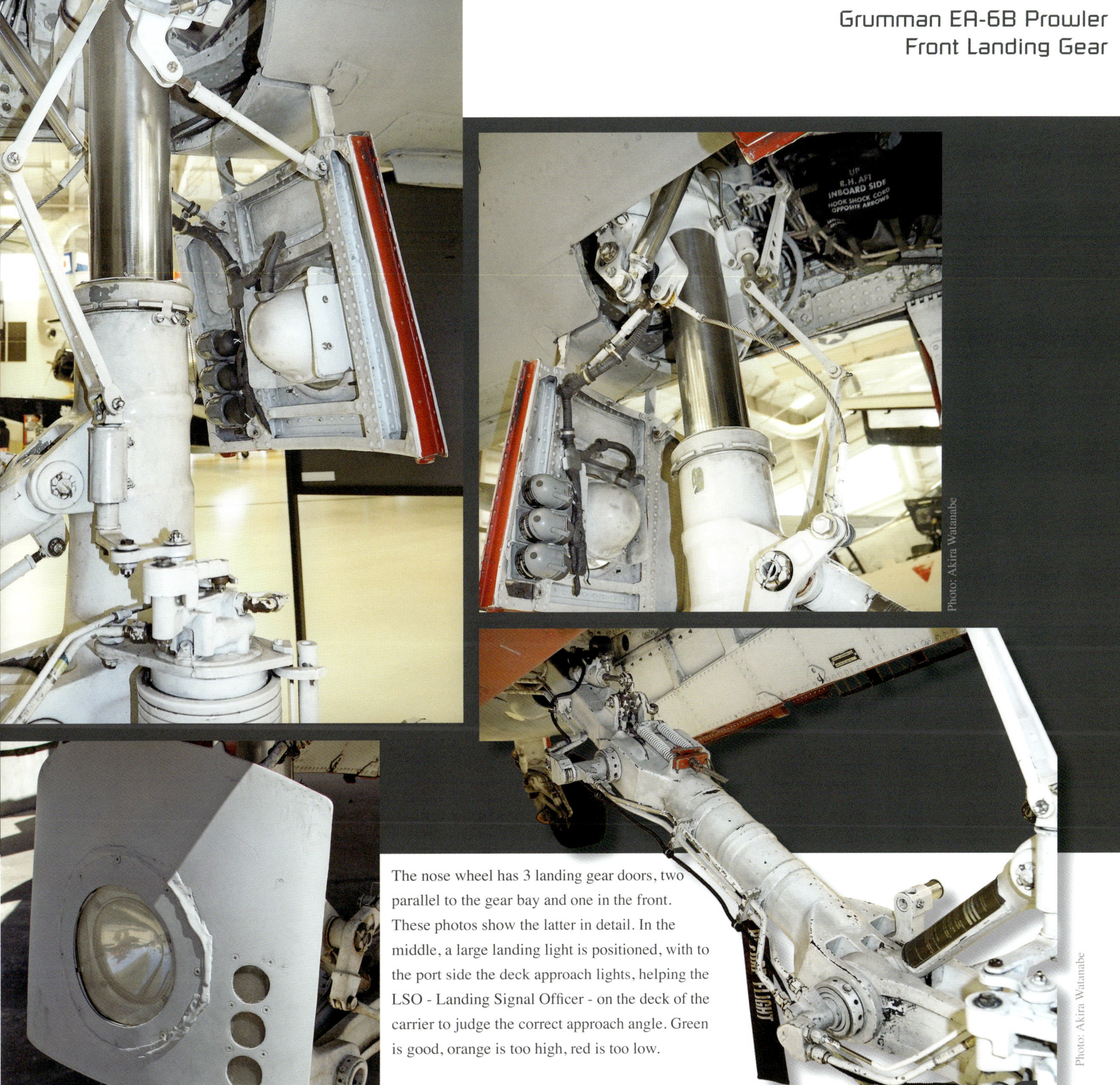

The nose wheel has 3 landing gear doors, two parallel to the gear bay and one in the front. These photos show the latter in detail. In the middle, a large landing light is positioned, with to the port side the deck approach lights, helping the LSO - Landing Signal Officer - on the deck of the carrier to judge the correct approach angle. Green is good, orange is too high, red is too low.

Photo: Akira Watanabe

Photo: Dave Cing

Photo: Akira Watanabe

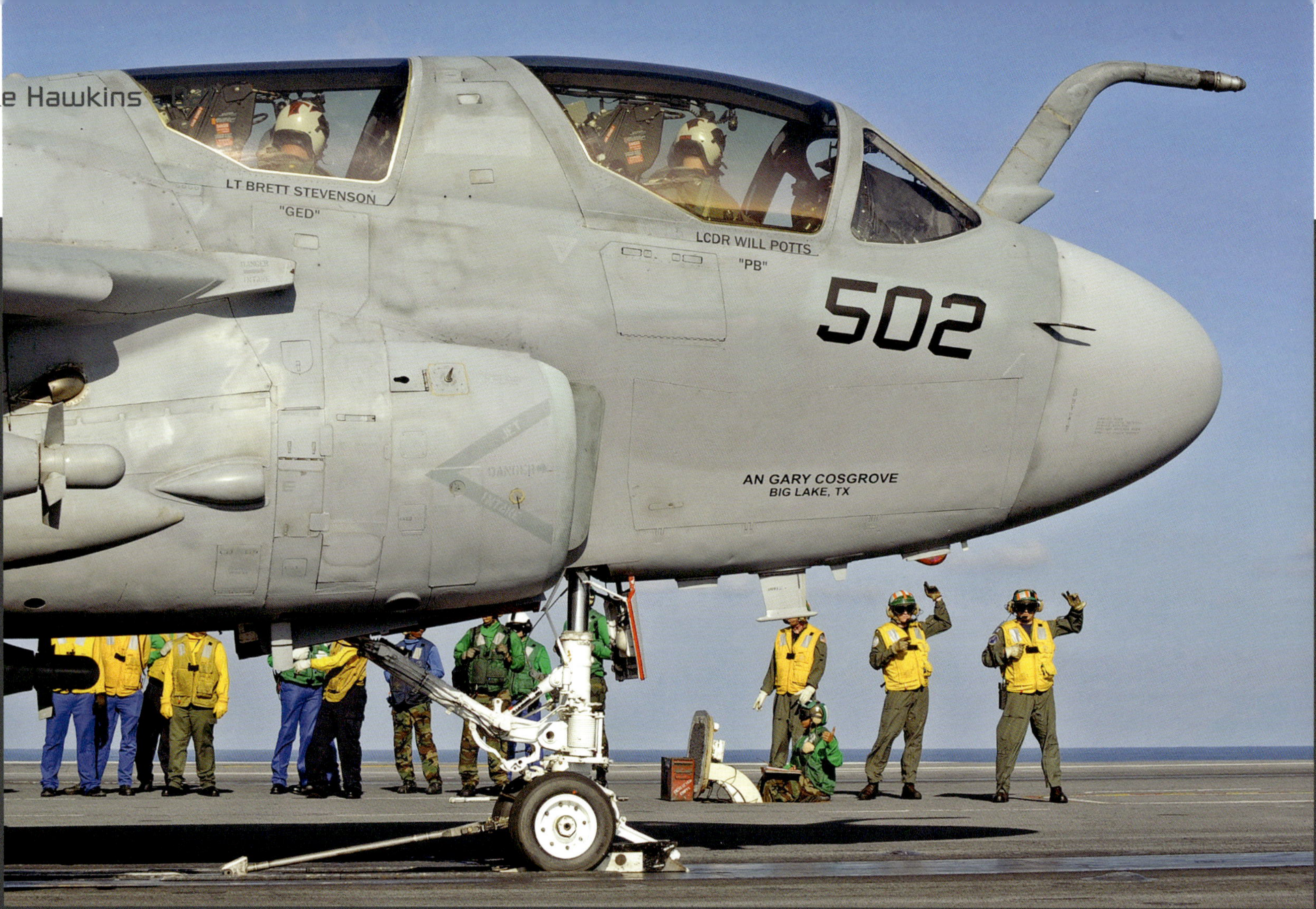

Above: This photo offers a good view at the nose gear connected to the catapult shuttle. Notice the holdback bar aft of the gear. Deck crew signal the status of the launch to the pilot. The two aft gear doors are just visible from this angle. Ged, PB and the two other crew members are about to be shot into the air in a mere 90 meters!

Right: A first look inside the cramped nose gear wheel bay. Look at all the wiring and pipes running in this area. The nose gear actuator pulls the main struts and wheels back into the wheel bay in a matter of seconds. Notice the red painted edges of the doors. To the left in the photo, the gear door actuators can be seen.

Photo: Akira Watanabe

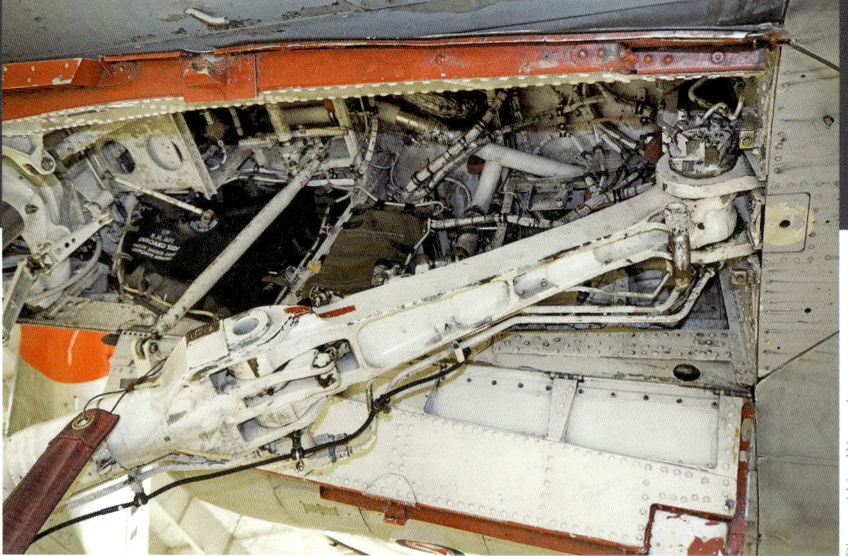

These photos show the forward landing gear bay from all sides. A pair of metal coloured containers are fixed to the port side of the bay. Notice the canvas cover on the starboard side of the bay. See where the gear door actuators are attached? The photo to the left is interesting, because you can see where the holdback bar is connected to the landing gear, exactly in between the two wheels. Look at the shimmy damper on the starboard side of the gear. The photo below was taken from the starboard side of the aircraft; look at the refuelling point.

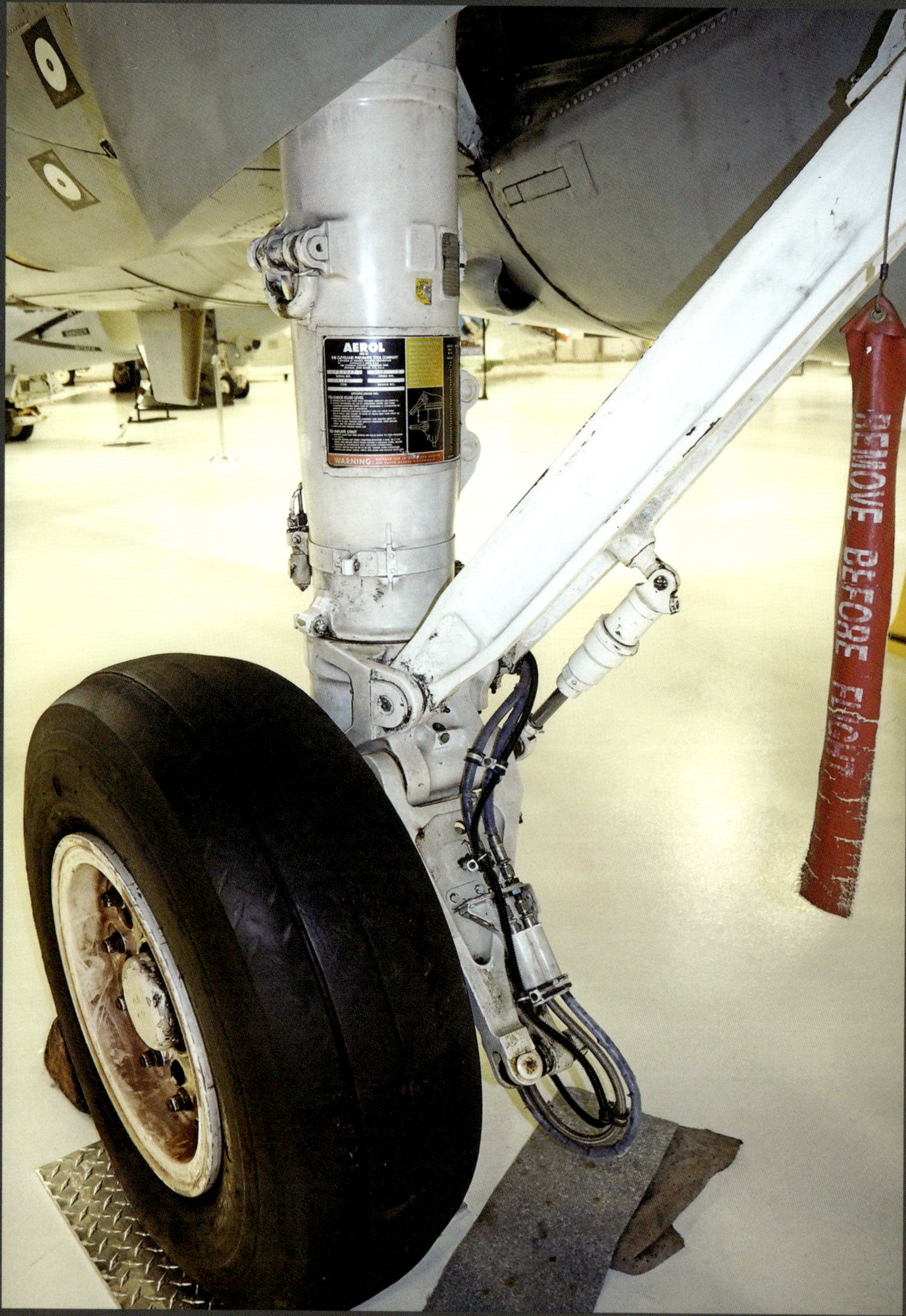

Photo: Akira Watanabe

Photo: Akira Watanabe

Photo: Akira Watanabe

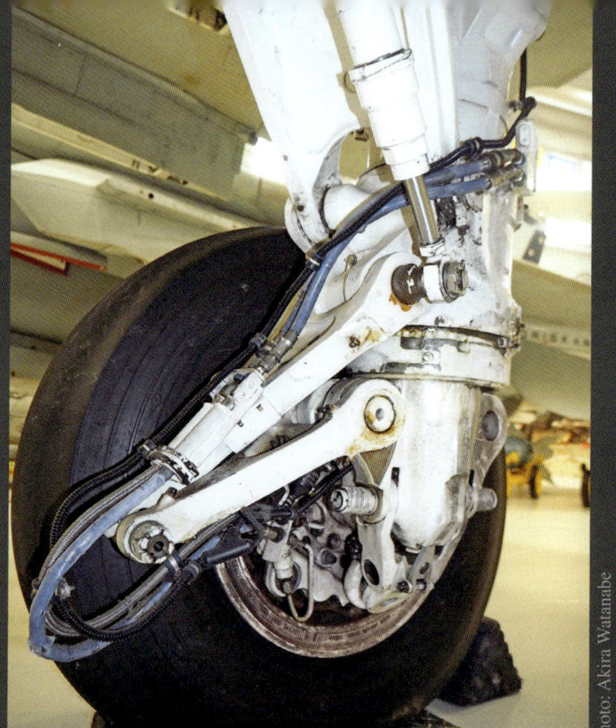

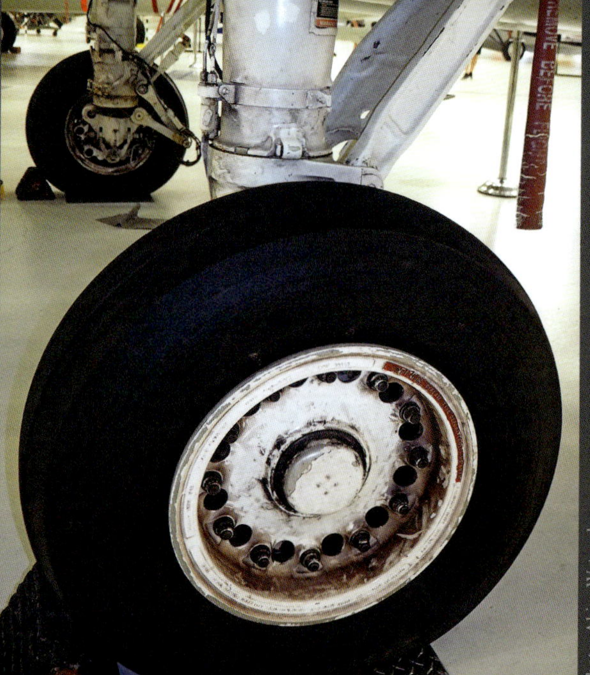

The main gear of the Prowler is as impressive as it is strong and resembles strongly the structure of the main gear of the F-14 Tomcat, another famous product of the Grumman Ironworks. The wheels on the main gear are slightly over 90 cm in diameter and 30 cm wide. They are positioned at the extremities of the fuselage, adding to the jet's stability.

Slats and flaps down, hook lowered; this EA-6B is about to slam on the deck of the USS Theodore Roosevelt. The main gear is fully extended and ready to take the shock. Each main gear is equipped with mutiple disk wheel brakes.

Right: This photo shows the forward main gear bay doors. Each gear has three doors, with the aft one horizontal, next to the main strut. On the ground, the doors are open, but once the aircraft powered up, the front two doors are closed, as can be seen in the photo above. The bulge on the upper door is so there is room for the door actuator folding mechanism. The two connected doors are retracted by means of a single actuator, located at the front.

Photo: Philip Stevens

Photo: Akira Watanabe

Photo: Kevin Whitehead

Above: This is a rather unusual photo of an EA-6B Prowler, because it doesn't have anything fixed to its wings or centreline. It gives a good idea of how high the aircraft actually stands on its landing gear. Notice that the two forward landing gear doors of the main gear are closed when the aircraft is powered up. It seems that someone on board is a motorcycle aficionado...

Right: The inside of the forward main gear door. with the actuator to the front. Notice the tubing running over it.

Photo: Akira Watanabe

Photo: Dave Chng

Photo: Dave Chng

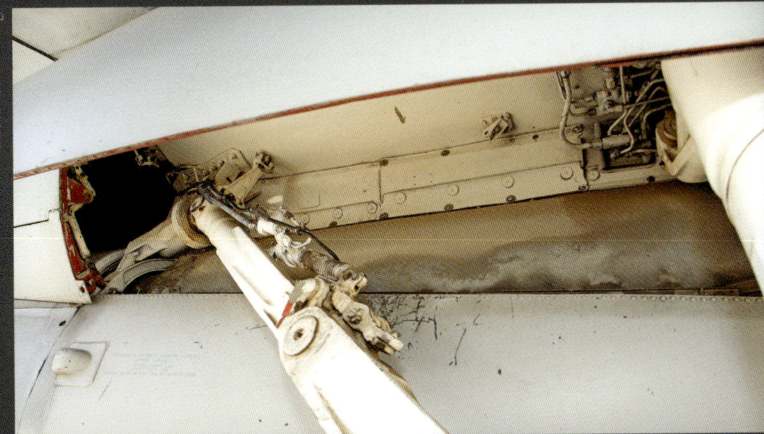

The main landing gear is pulled forward during retraction, with the wheel turning almost 90 degrees to a horizontal position to fit into the wheel bay. These photos show where the impressive actuator is connected to the fuselage. Look at all the tubes and wires inside the wheel bays.

Photo: Dave Chng

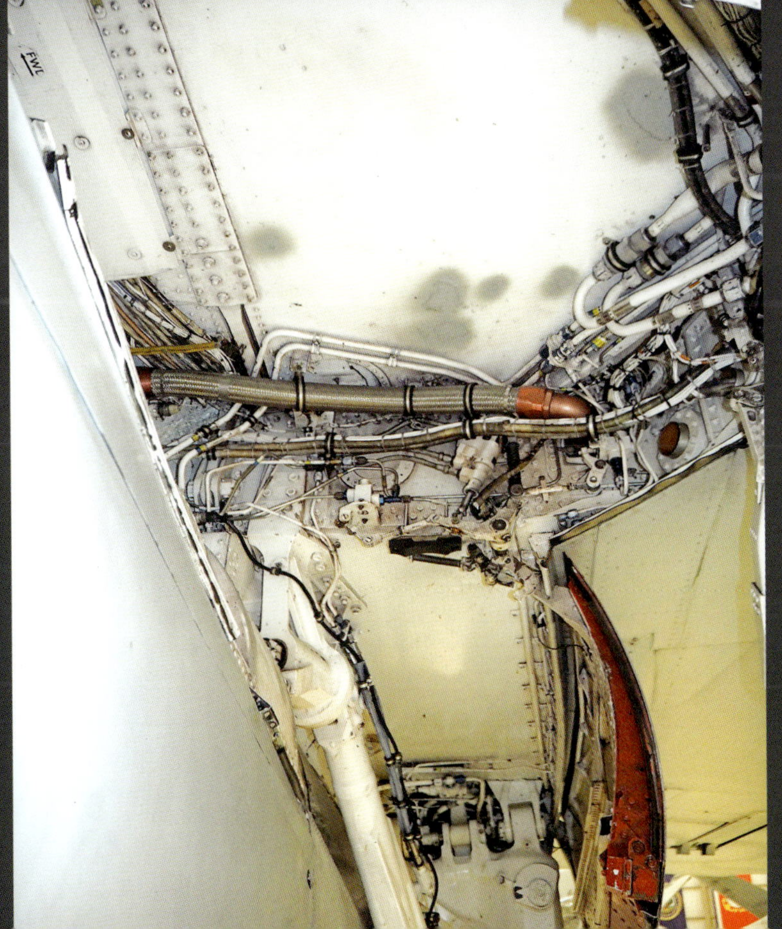

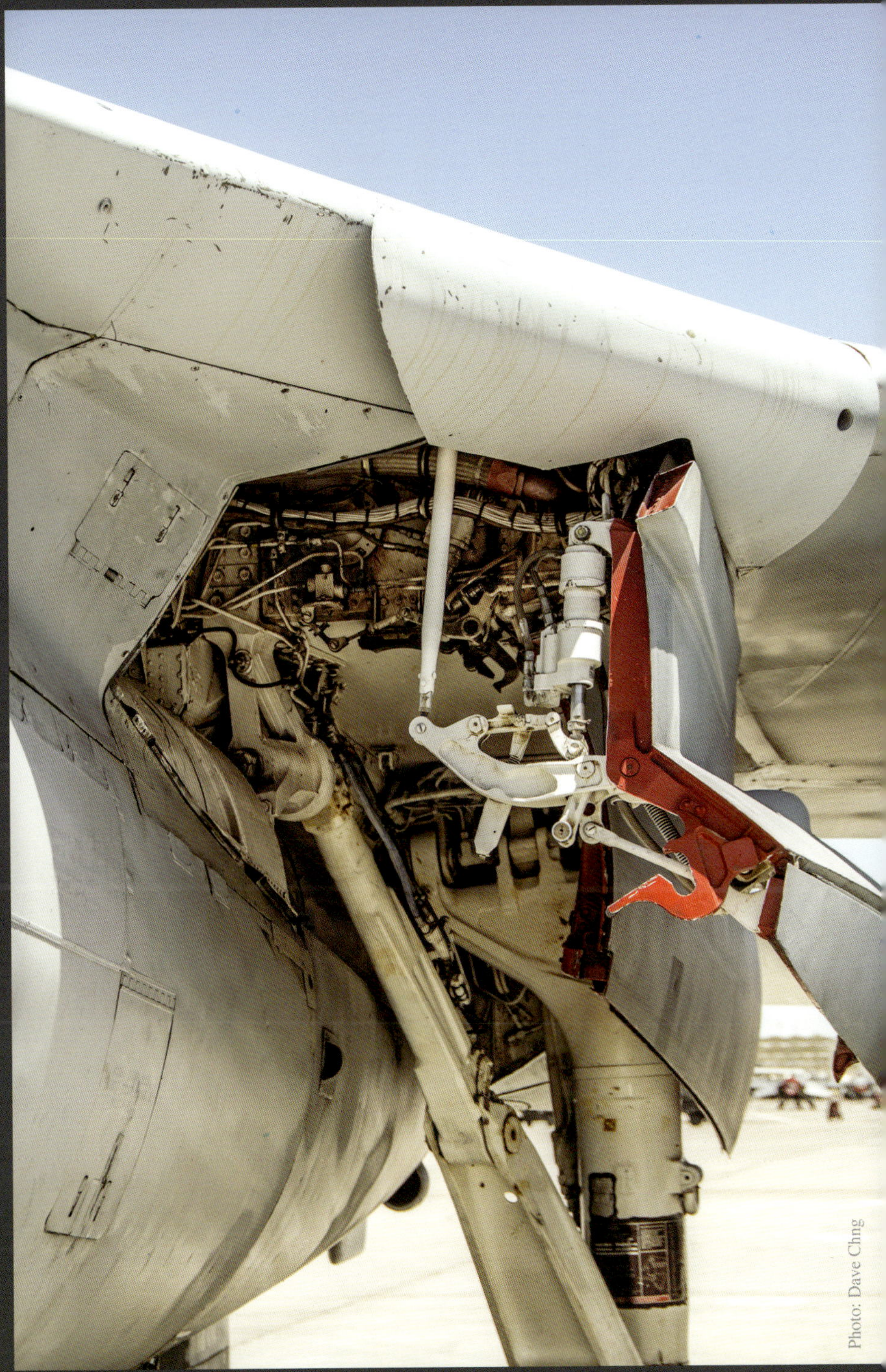

Photo: Dave Chng

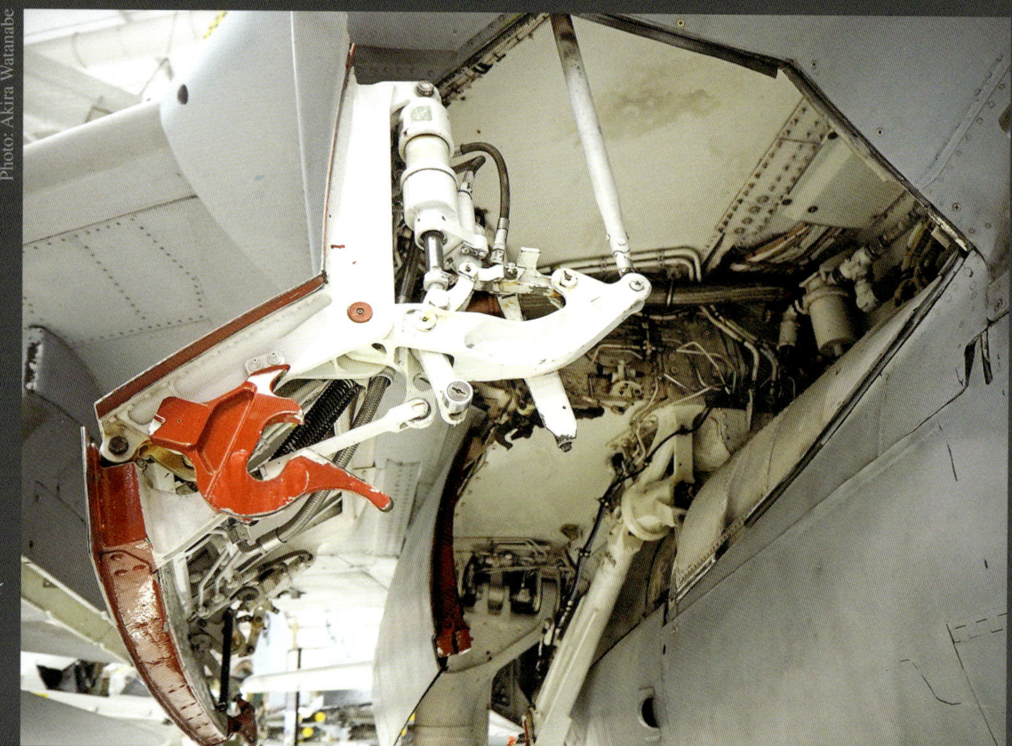

Left: The actuator system of the forward main wheel bay doors. Again, the edges of these parts are painted bright red.

Below: The third main gear bay door of the starboard gear, seen from the front. This door has a hydraulic actuator at the rear of the door. Notice the structure on the inside of the door and where the main strut fits into the bay ceiling.

Photo: Akira Watanabe

Above: The starboard bay, looking forward. The shape of the lower part of the bay follows the shape of the air intake. Look at the cover at the ceiling, protecting wires.

Photo: Joe Copalman

Above: Smoke blasts of the main gear tires when this Prowler slams onto the runway. Another very cool shot from Joe Copalman. From this angle, you can see how wide the landing gear of the EA-6B actually is. The slats are competely lowered at 27,5 degrees.

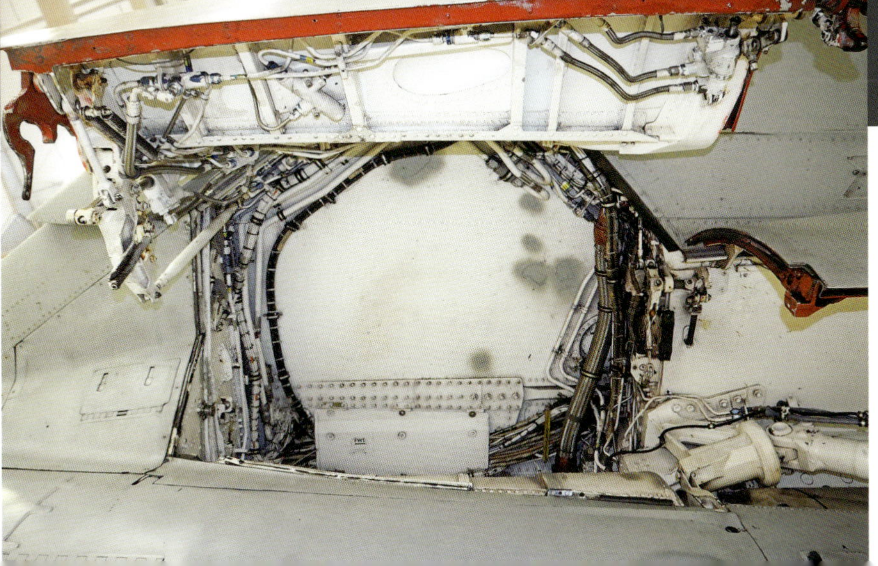

Photo: Akira Watanabe

Photo: Dave Chng

This profile of the Prowler shows the many antennas located all around the aircraft. From the base of the vertical fin runs a horizontal strake which houses the AN/ARC-105 HF radio antenna. Notice the low band antenna blisters located on the vertical tail.

Right: This photo shows the lower aft fuselage of the Prowler. The large fin is the AN/USQ-113 Communications Jammer Antenna. It is placed on the aft avionics bay, which folds down for easy access. In it, the "birdcage" or Extensible Equipment Platform is located, where avionics and black boxes are stowed. Notice the chaf/flare dispencer opening located immediately behind it.

Photo: Dave Chng

Above: The AN/ASQ-113 Communications Jammer antenna, located in front of the arrestor hook seen from the front.

Right: A close-up of the aft port fuselage of a Prowler of the "Seahawks". Near the top of the A of Marines a gauge is located, which indicated the pneumatic pressure of the arresting gear. Look at the oil streaks coming from the rivets.

A Marines Prowler is about to land after a training mission. From this angle, a lot of the antennas on the spine and aft fuselage can be seen. Notice the position of the horizontal tails. The three white antennas on the spine were introduced with the ICAP II upgrade and are part of the modified electronics suite. The air scoop on the starboard side provides cold air for the avionics and jamming equipment. Above the national insignia, formation strips are placed.

Photo: Philip Stevens

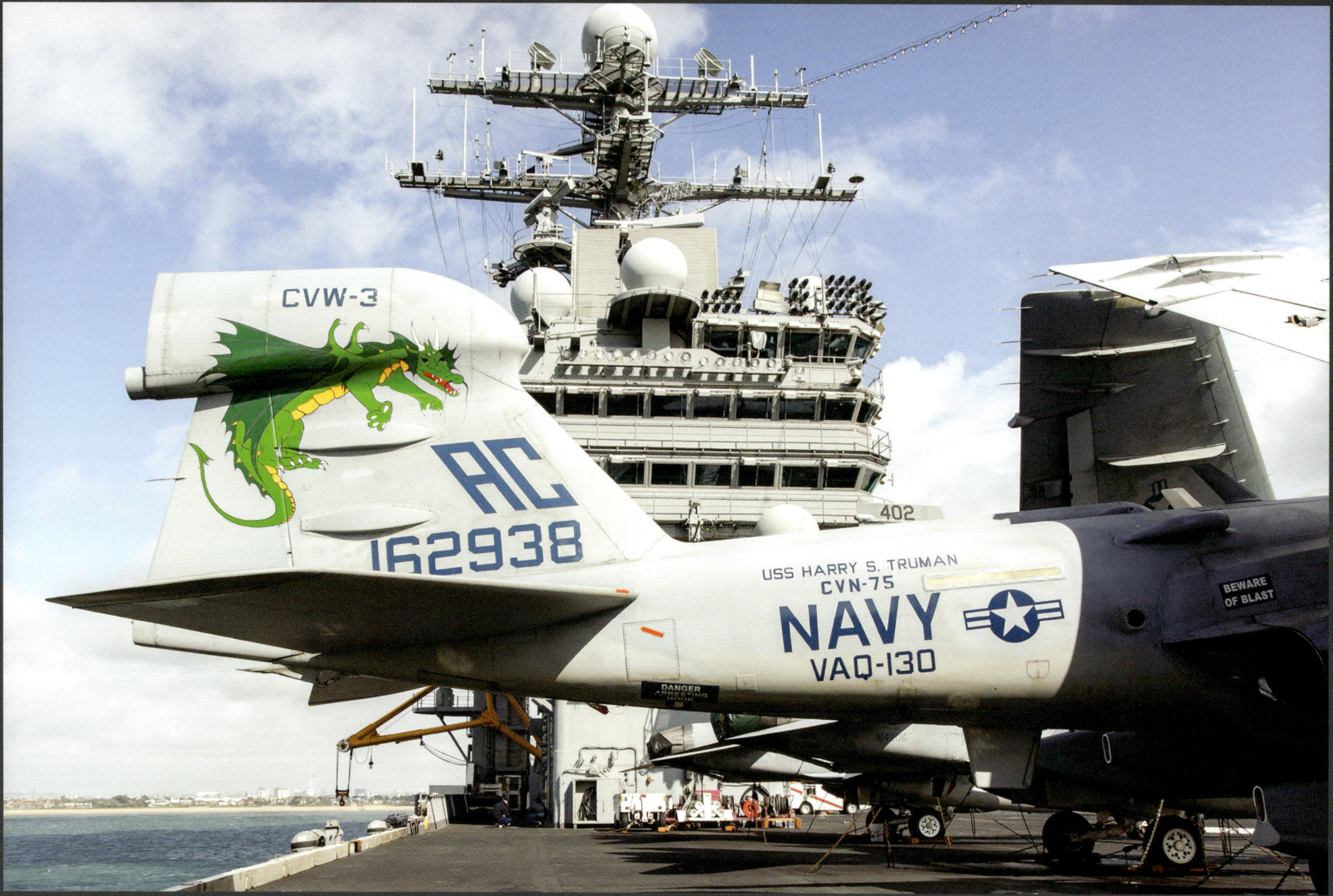

Above: Here's a tailmarking that would be approved by Daenerys Targaryen herself! The vertical tail of the EA-6B is dominated by the large ECM pod on top of it, which is often referred to as the Football. It houses countermeasures receivers. On the trailing edge of the pod, the AN/ALQ-126 Noise Deception Jammer is located, which is known as the Beercan. On the starboard side of the fuselage, just aft of the engine exhaust, the aft cooling turbine exhaust for the electronical equipment is located. Look at the size of the ventral AN/ASQ-113 Communications Jammer antenna.

Photo: US Navy

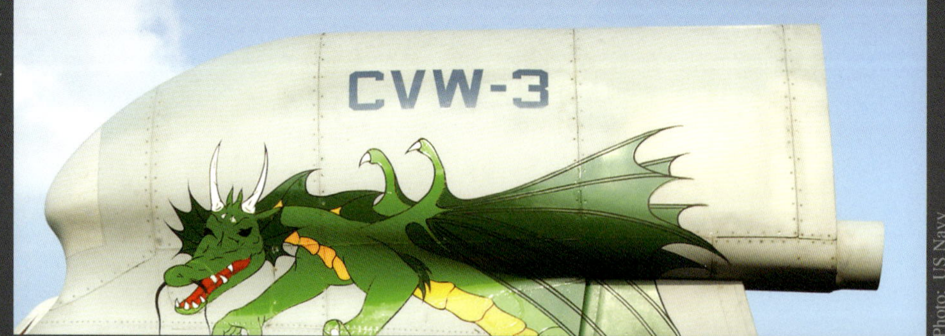

Photo: Dave Chng

Photo: Akira Watanabe

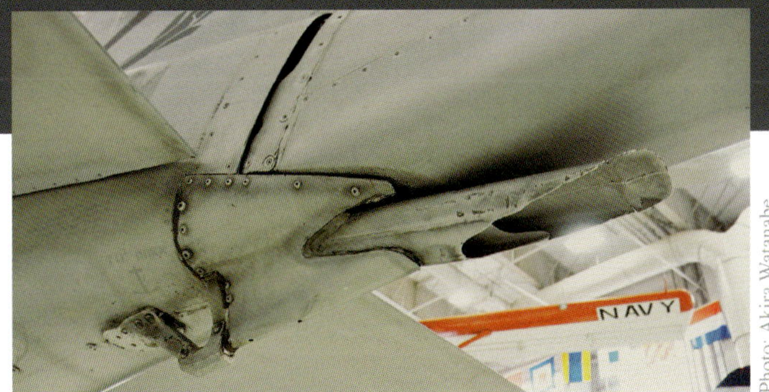

Photo: Akira Watanabe

Above: Below the rudder of the vertical tail, a fuel vent is located.

Notice the tie down point in front of it.

Above: This EA-6B of the "Banshees" is loaded with a pair of AGM-88 HARM missiles. With a length of over 4 meter, they are pretty impressive.

Right: A close-up of the Football. Notice that the Beercan is missing from the trailing edge.

Photo: Akira Watanabe

Grumman EA-6B Prowler
Vertical Tail

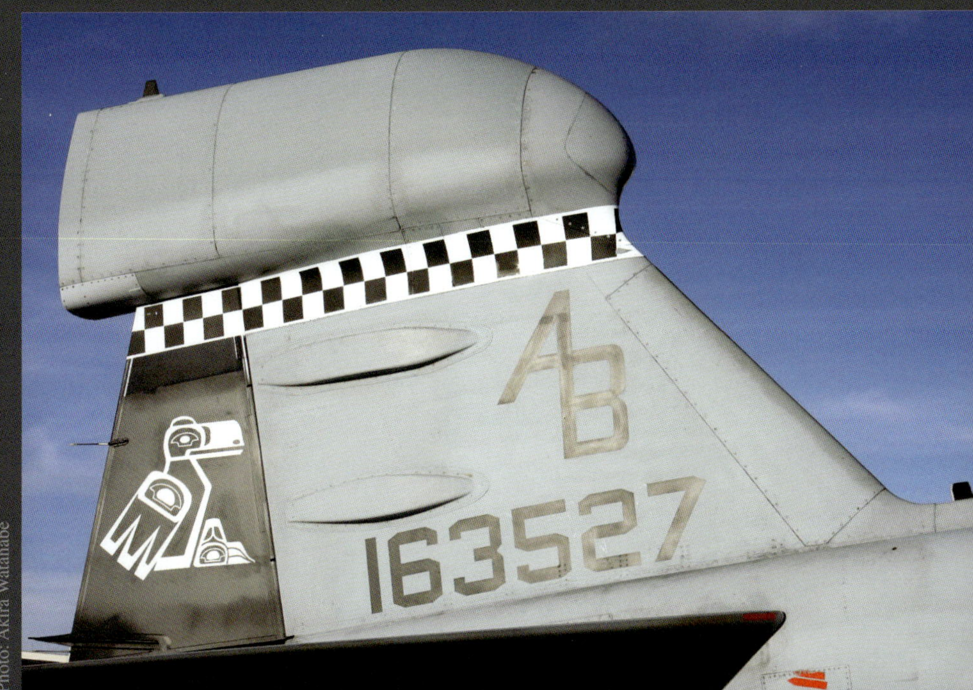

Photo: Akira Watanabe

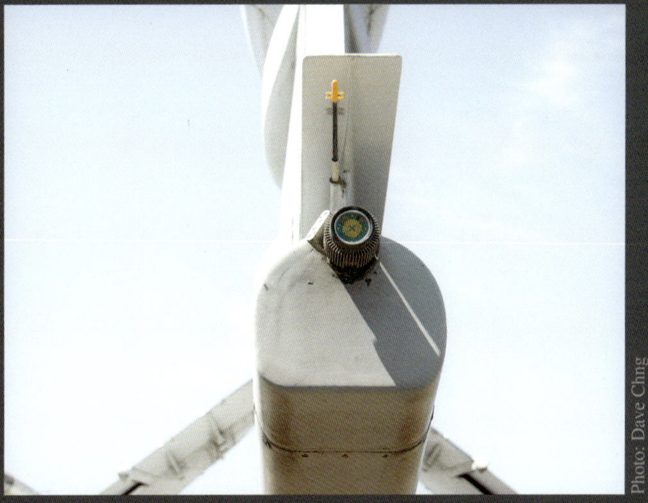

Photo: Dave Chng

Left: The vertical tail with the ECM pod, blisters on the side and the rudder at the trailing edge. Notice the single static discharger fixed to it.
Above: Underneath the Signal Interference plate, which was introduced with the ICAP II upgrade, a navigation light is fixed.

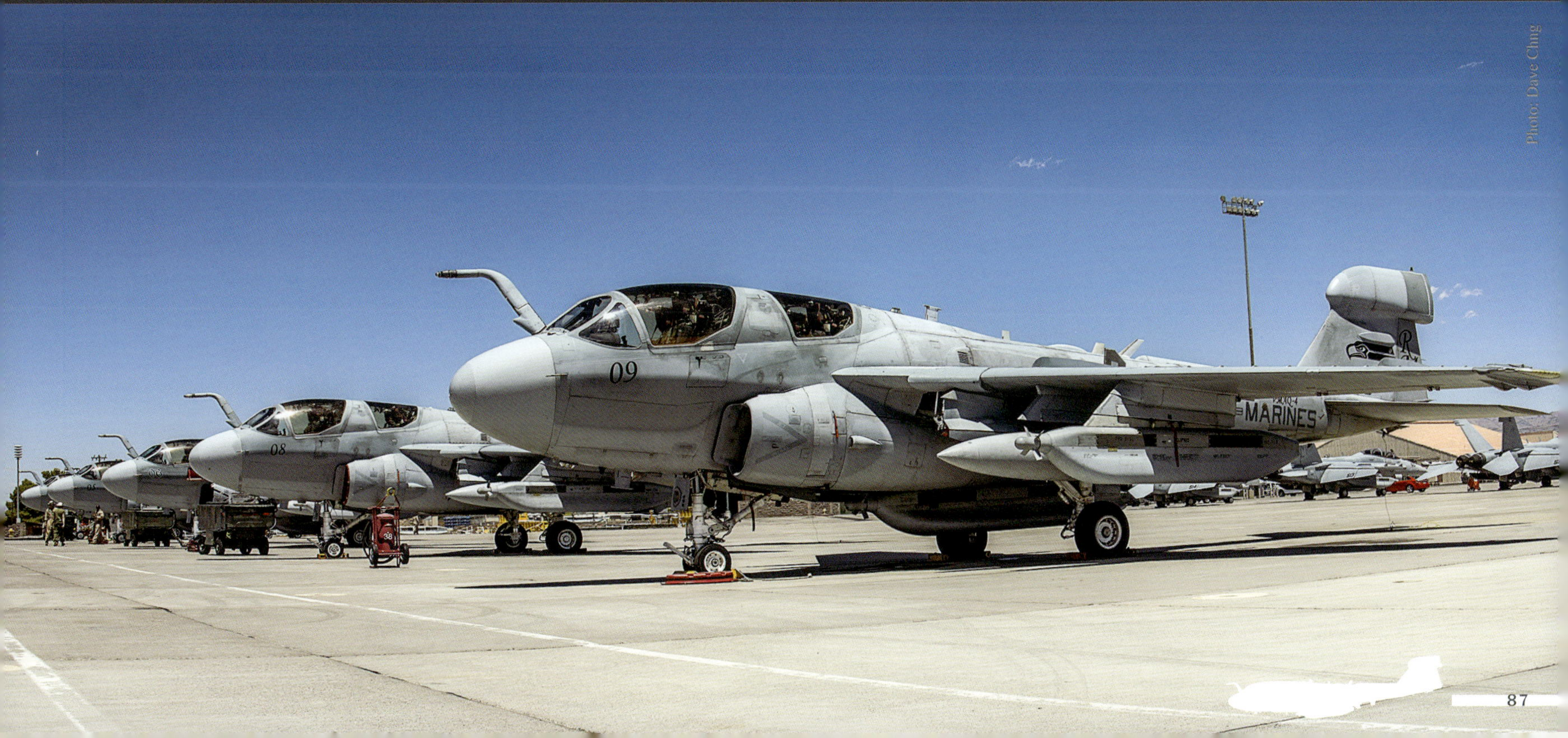

Photo: Dave Chng

Above: Wham! A Gray Wolf slams on the deck after a mission. While smoke is coming from the nose gear wheels, the arrestor hook snaps up the last of the 4 cables on the deck. Notice the position of the slats and speed brakes.

Left: The arrestor hook, looking upwards. The hook has a strengthened Y-shape. Notice the pair of chaff/flare dispencers located in between the fuselage connections points.

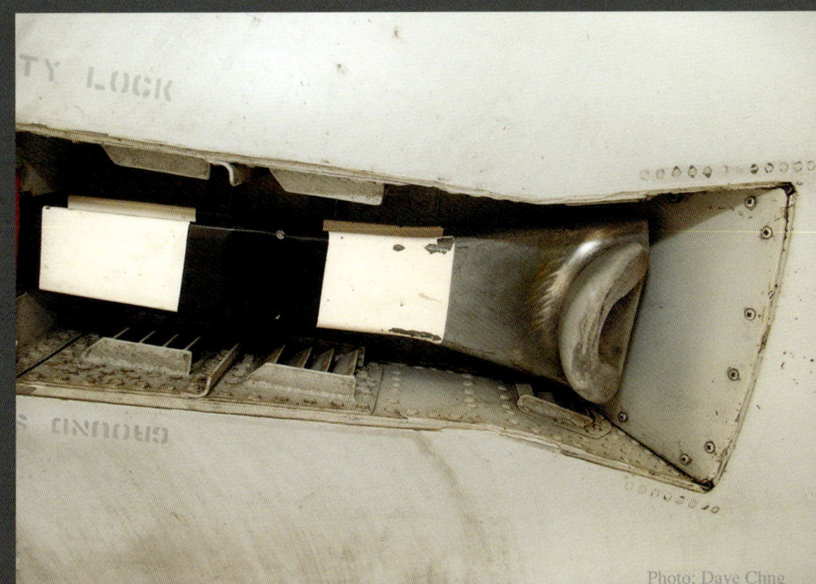

The aft part of the arrestor hook is painted black and white. The hook is pretty heavy, which is needed when you have to try to stop an aircraft weighing over 20 tons! The photo above shows the hook fixed with a red painted Ground Safety Lock.

Above: An EA-6B Prowler is being shot off the USS Nimitz at the same time as a Super Hornet, which blasts off from one of the bow catapults. To the right, legacy Hornets are parked, with the one in front waiting to taxi towards the catapult.

Right: A pair of EA-6B Prowlers of VAQ-139 Cougars on patrol. The position and the swept angle of the horizontal tails are apparent in this photo. Look at the weathering of the engine bay panels. The EA-6B has a maximum take off weight of just under 28 tons. The cruising speed of the Prowler is 650 km/h with an impressive range of 3,745 km, without in-flight refuelling.

Photo: Kevin Whitehead

Left: This Prowler is the CAG bird of VAQ-129 "Vikings". It is banking hard to the left, providing an excellent view of the wings and horizontal tails. Notice the details of the top fuselage and how far forward the base of the vertical tail extends. Look at the different shade of grey of the walkways.

Akira Watanabe

Photo: Stephan Ortmann

Above: The starboard horizontal tail of a "Zapper". These stabilizers are all moving and hydraulically operated. Red markings at the leading edge and fuselage indicate when it is exactly horizontal. The vertical tail of the aicraft stands pretty high at 5,08 meter.

Photo: Dave Chng

Above: The base of the horizontal tails. At the far end of the fuselage, a fuel vent is located.

Maintaining the Prowler

Time to get into the maintenance hangar. The Grumman EA-6B Prowler is a specialist in its field and much appreciated, but the downside is that it needs quite a bit of maintenance. Remember that the aircraft has a design going back to the final years of the 1950s - the first flight of the A-6 Intruder was in April 1960. This chapter is always one of my favorites, because it shows a lot of otherwise hidddn details but also because it is in honour of the technicians, mechanics and engineers that make sure these aircraft can stay operational and in the best possible condition. At the beginning of the year 2000, there were 104 Prowlers flying with the US Navy and US Marines and in order to keep the aircraft flying, the most extensive maintenance tasks were the replacement of the Wing Center Section and the Standard Depot Level Maintenance. However, when an aircraft was schedules for this, it also removed it for 10 to 12 months from the inventory. This, combined with shortages of some equipment, made it a huge challenge for the maintenance crews. Concequently, a program was developped to optimise the time an aircraft stayed in maintenance, thus keeping as many of them operational in a time when the Prowler was called upon constantly. The fantastic photo to the right shows a Prowler undergoing some serious maintenance: the engines have been removed, the ejection seats as well and numerous panels on the fuselage have been taken off. Now there's a diorama for the modellers among you!

Photo: Dave Chng

Photo: David Draycott

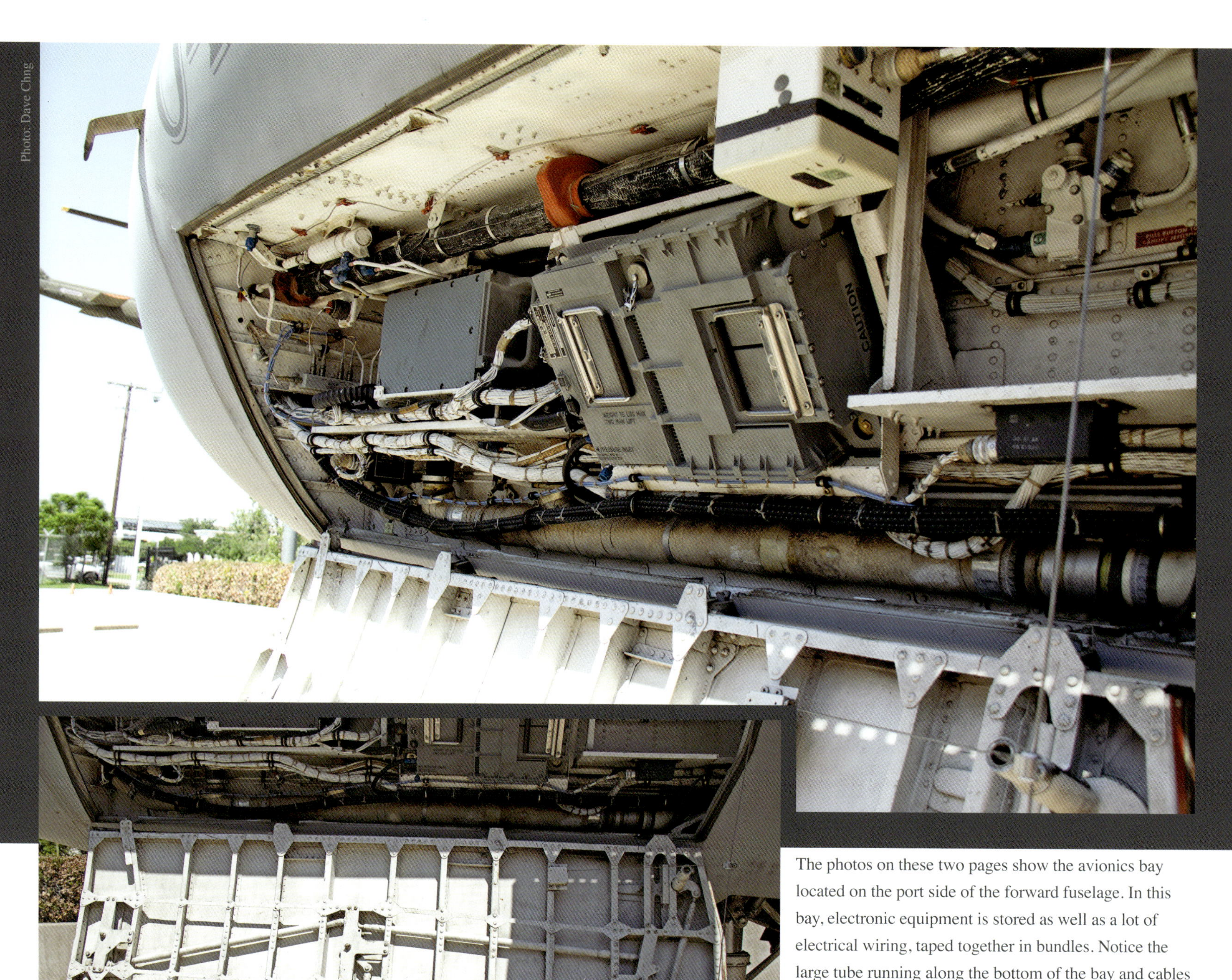

The photos on these two pages show the avionics bay located on the port side of the forward fuselage. In this bay, electronic equipment is stored as well as a lot of electrical wiring, taped together in bundles. Notice the large tube running along the bottom of the bay and cables coming from the AN/APS-130 Search Radar, located underneath the radome.

Left: The large single-piece avionics door and the mechanism fixing it to the fuselage, seen in detail.

More close-ups of the port avionics bay. During the ICAP II upgrade, many of the aircraft's systems were replaced with faster performing avionics. The AYA-6 computer was replaced with the advanced AN/AYK-14 and an AN/ASN Carrier Inertial Navigation System was installed. With the introduction of the TACAN, it was possible for the Prowlers to operate in pairs and cover a wider band of jamming frequencies and area.

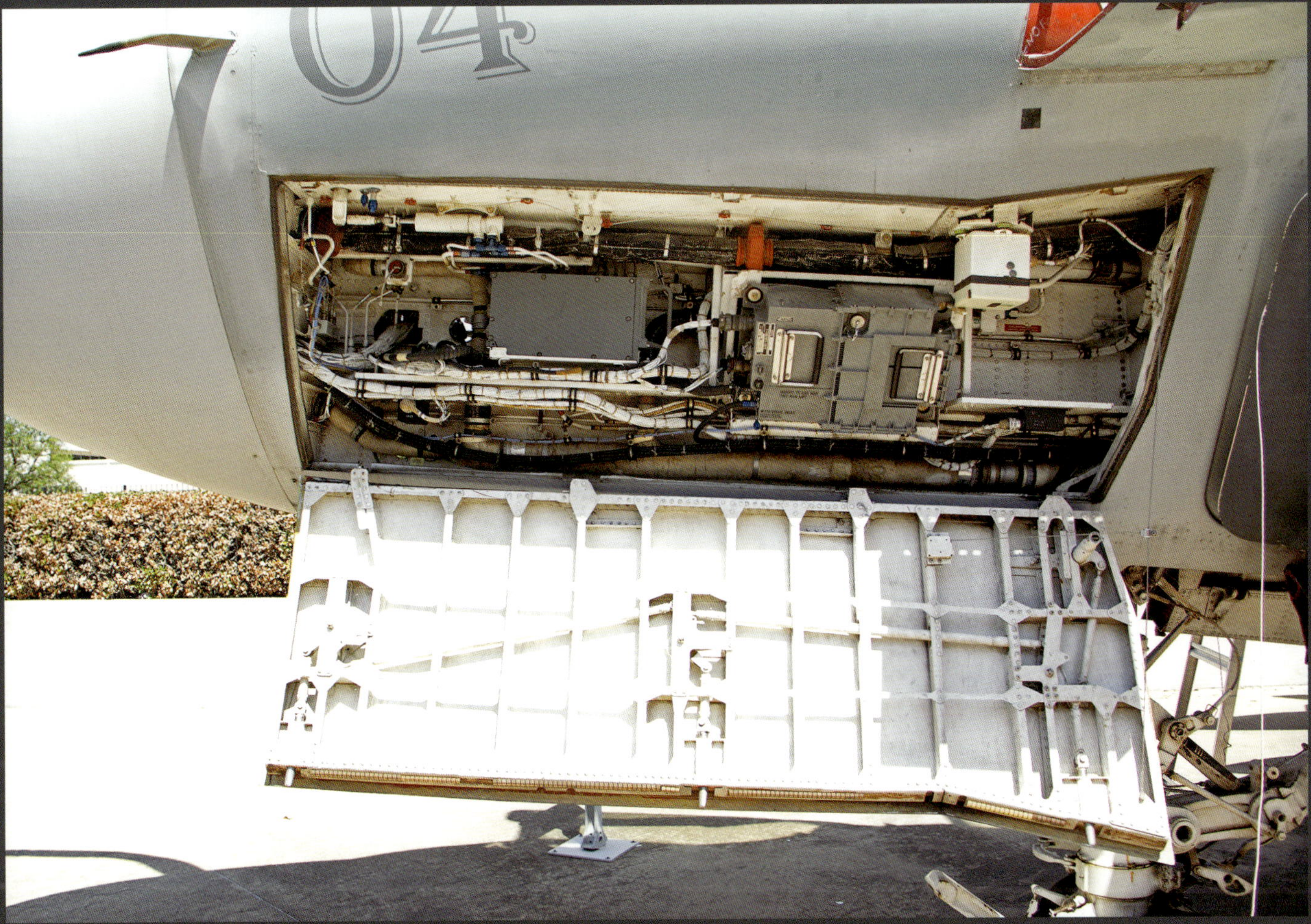

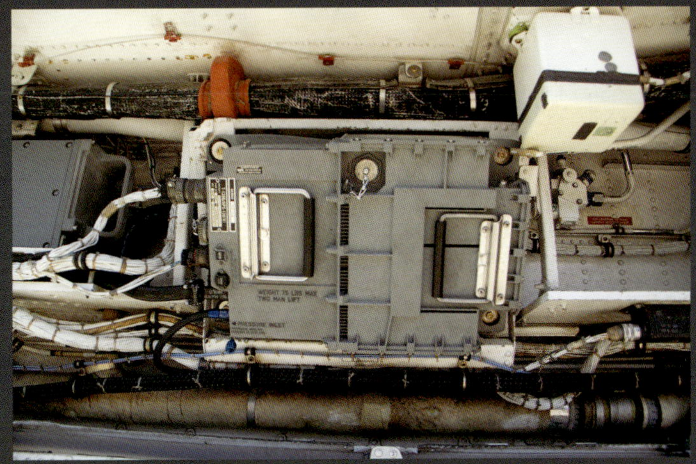

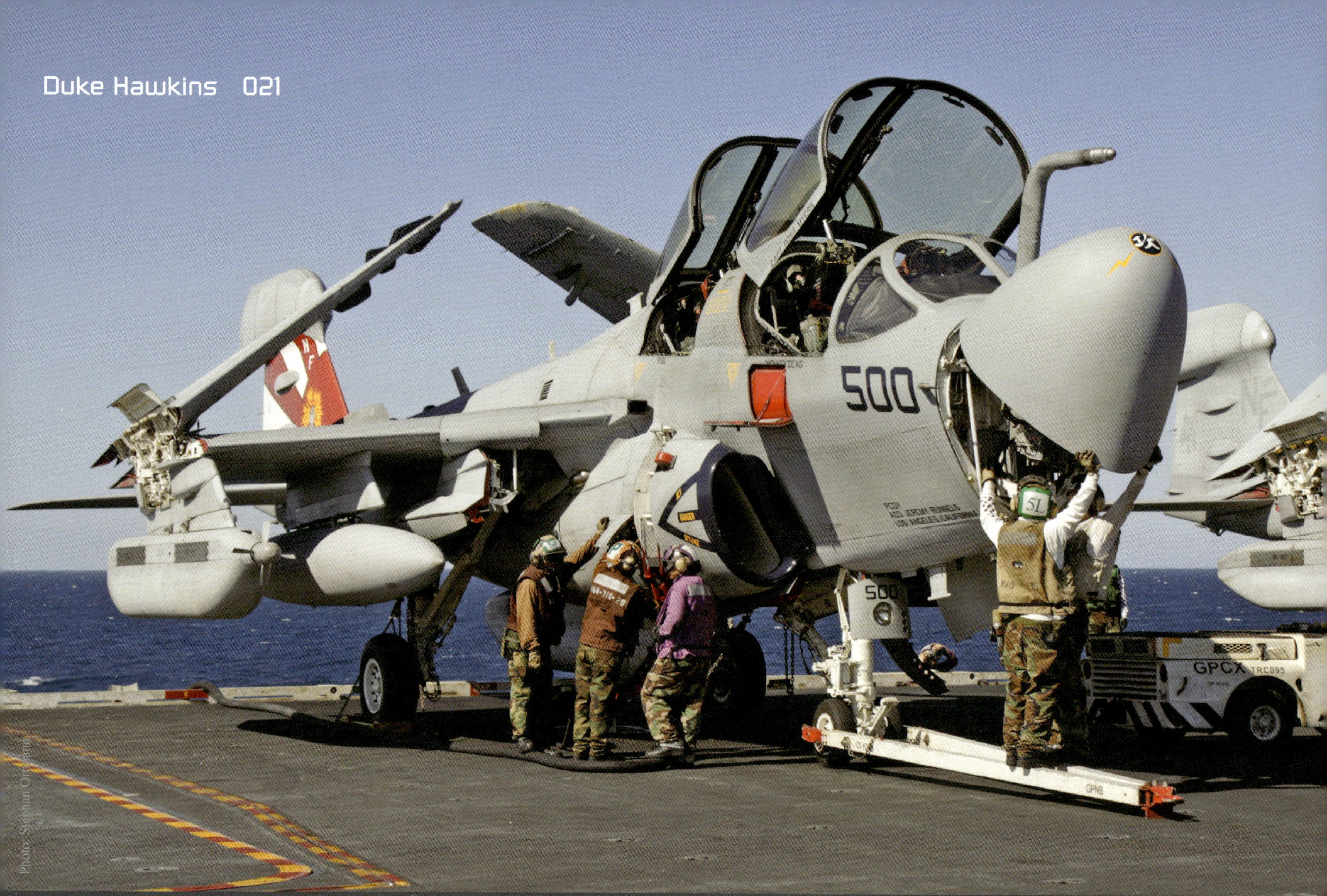

Photo: Stephan Ortmann

Above: Deck crew are doing a quick check on this Prowler of VAQ-136, "Gauntlets". The radome has been lifted to check the radar equipment. The Prowler played a vital role to keep the other aircraft of the aircraft carrier safe from enemy fire, which is why maintenance crew do whatever is necessary to keep them in perfect condition. In 2010, VAQ-136 was awarded the Golden Wrench Award for maintenance excellence by the Commander of the Naval Air Forces.

Right: Close-ups of the starboard avionics bay.

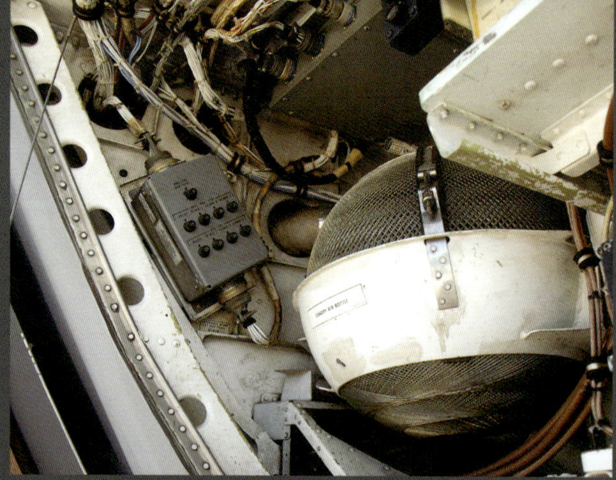

Photo: Dave Chng

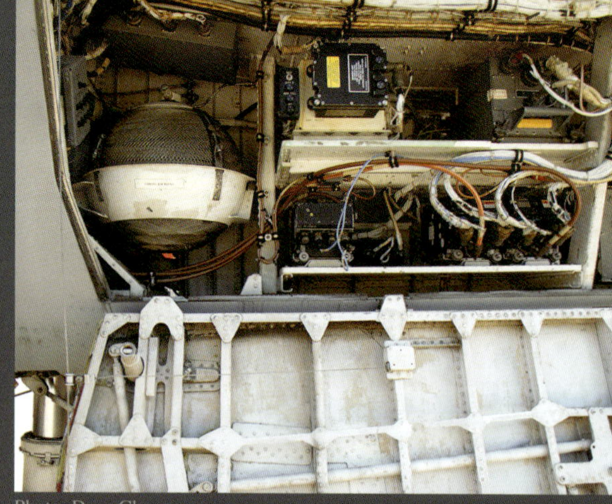

Photo: Dave Chng

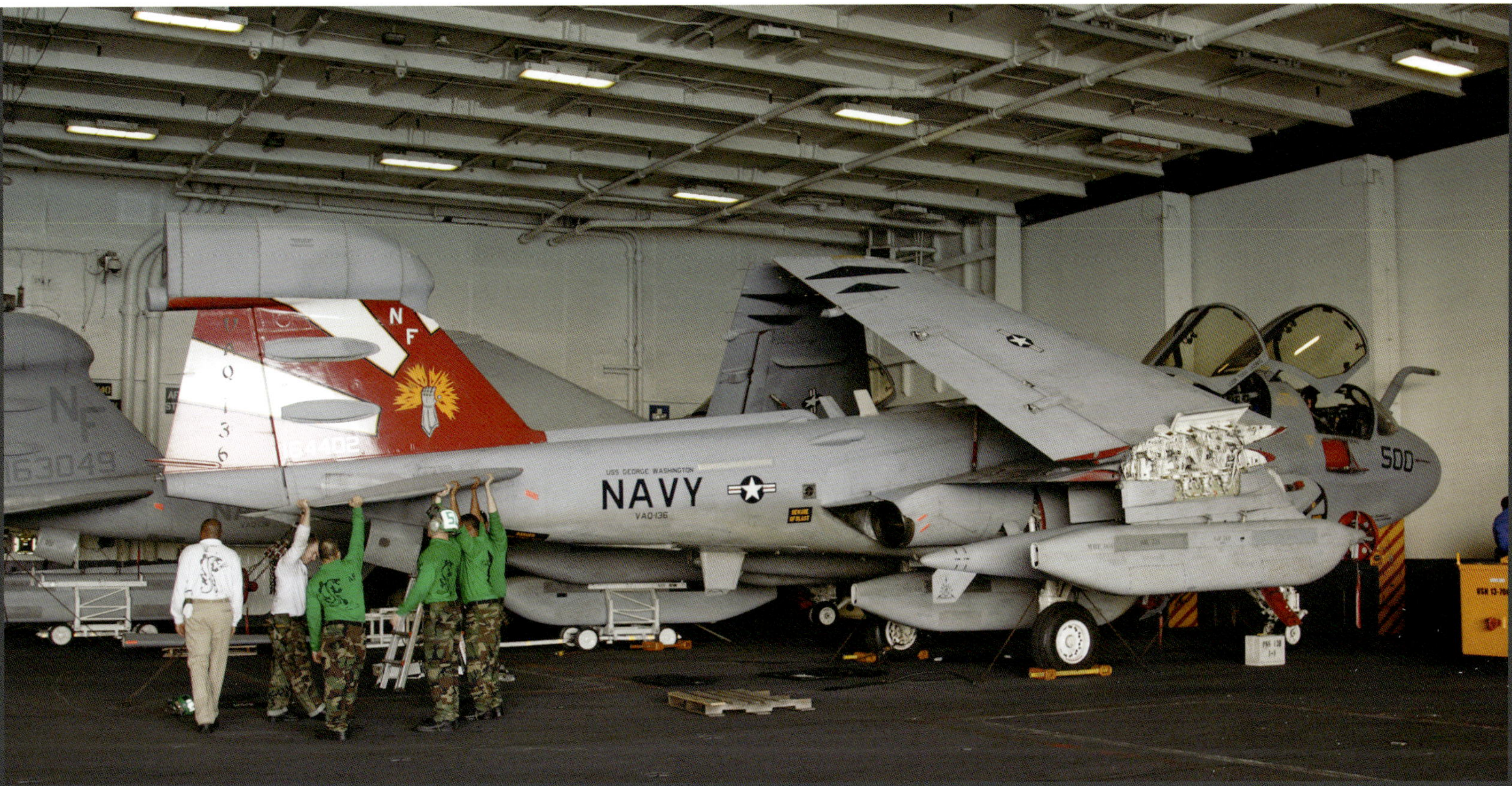

Photo: Stephan Ortmann

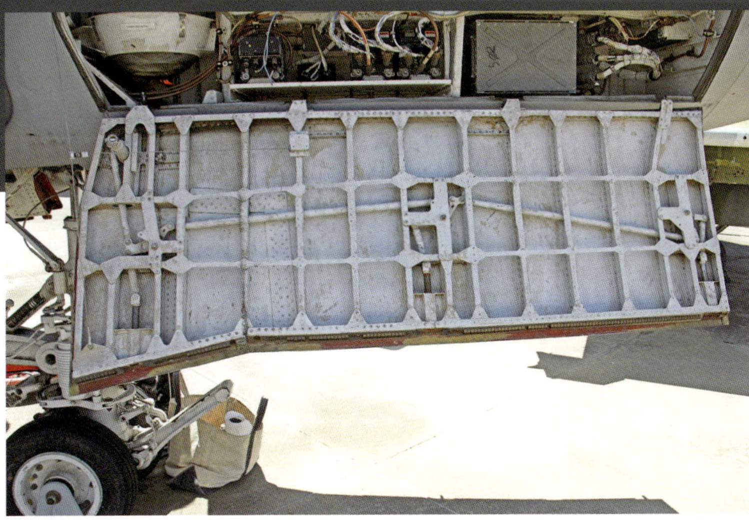

Below: The large access door to the starboard avionics bay in detail. Notice the mechanism that secures the door in to the hinges on the fuselage.

Photo: Dave Chng

Photo: Dave Chng

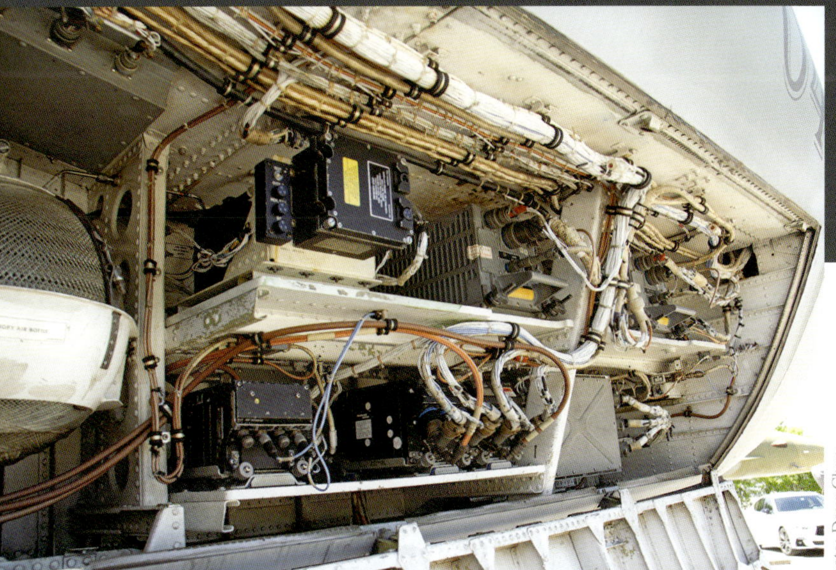

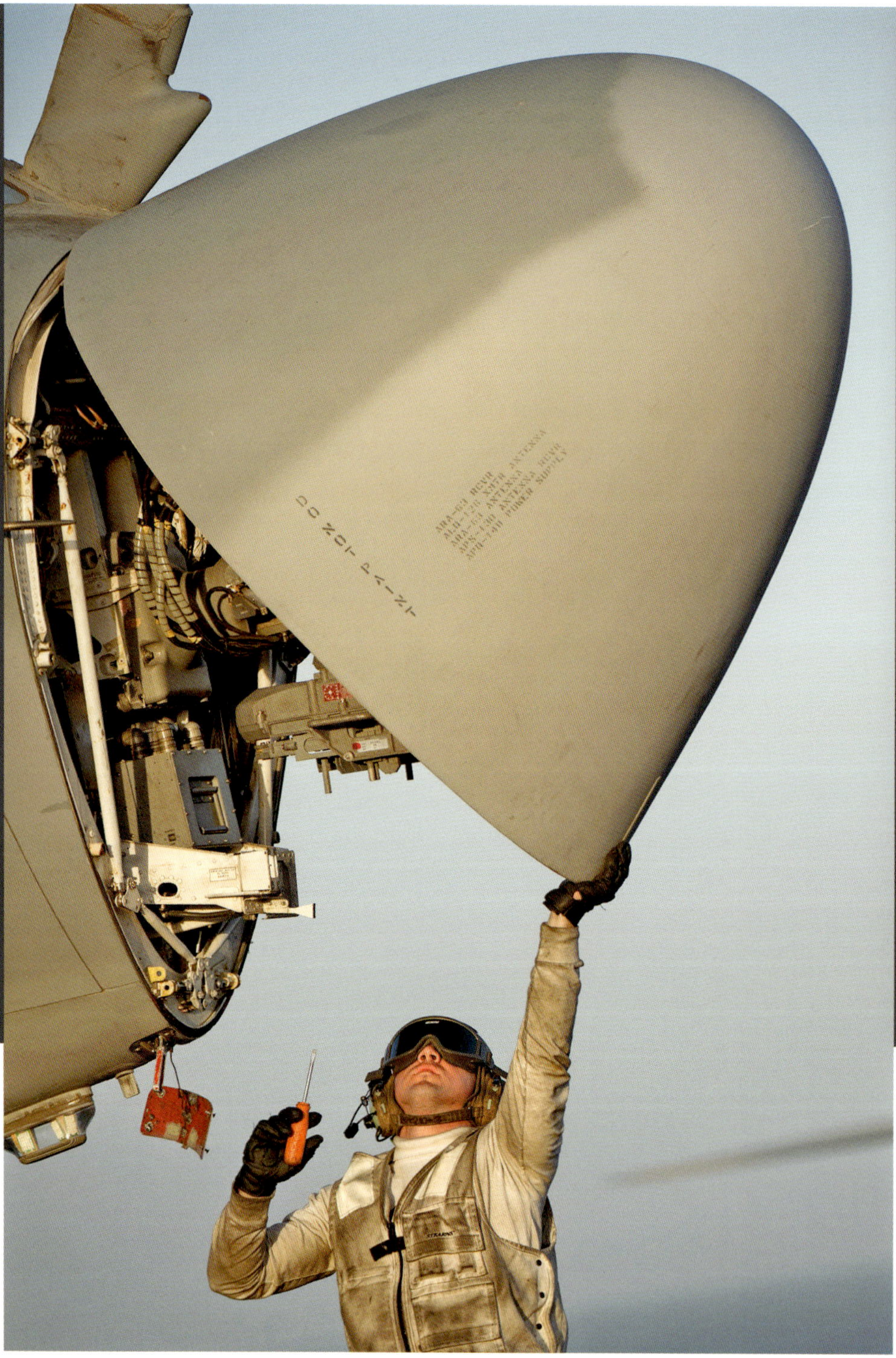

Photo: US Navy

Left: A quick look under the aircraft's radome to check a part of the radar. Look at the holding bar to the left in the photo.

Right: Immediately aft of the boarding ladder, in front of the air scoop on the air intake, this access door is located with the ground power circuit braker panel. It is opened by means of two simple push buttons. The photo below shows the Electrical Power systems check above the circuit braker panel.

Photo: Dave Chng

Photo: Dave Chng

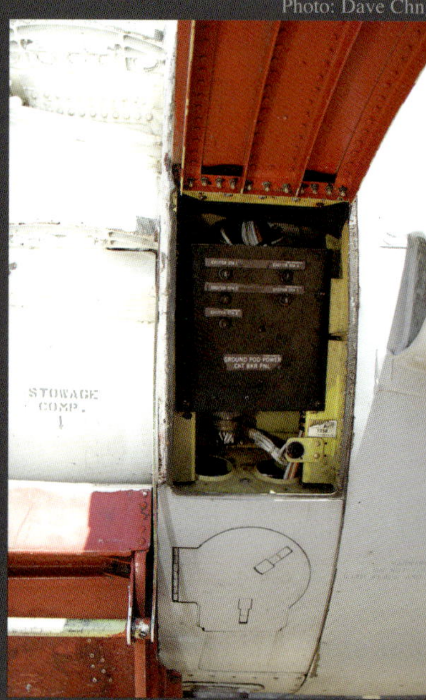

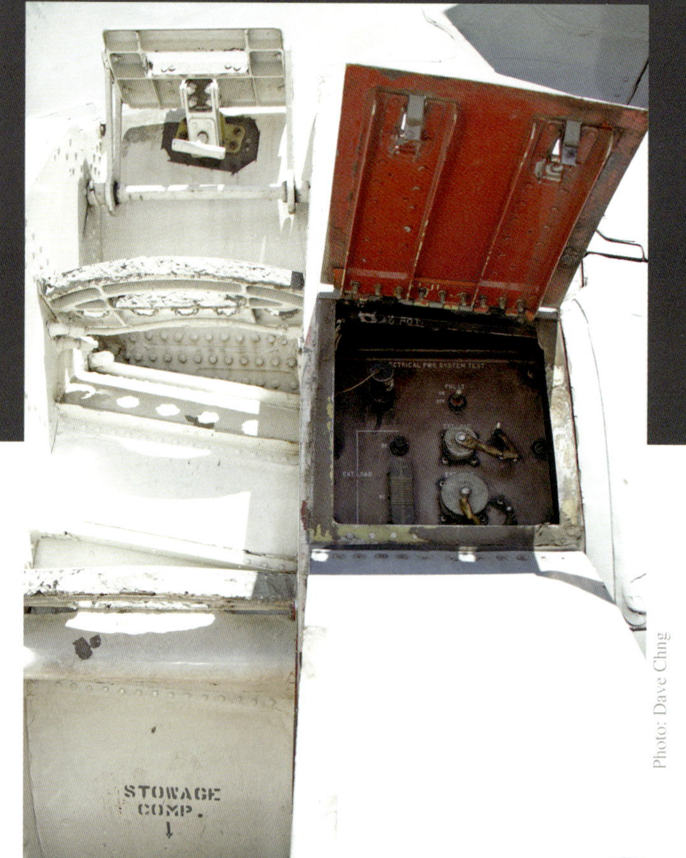

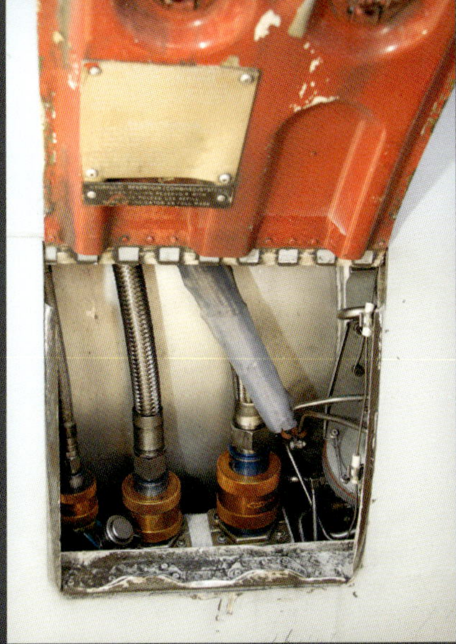

Left: Immediately below the main landing gear bay on the port side of the aircraft, this access panel can be found. The hydraulics systems can be checked here.

Below: The panel behind the aft cockpit on the port side has been removed to check the cabling and avionics inside. See where the panel above is located?

Above: Maintenance going on on an EA-6B Prowler, assigned to the "Gray Wolves" - VAQ-142, - on the flight deck of the USS Nimitz. The spine of the aircraft has been opened-up to check some of the tubes and connections. Below it is the large mid-fuselage fuel tank. The Prowler carries some 14,000 lbs of fuel internally, while another 10,000 lbs can be carried in external fuel tanks.

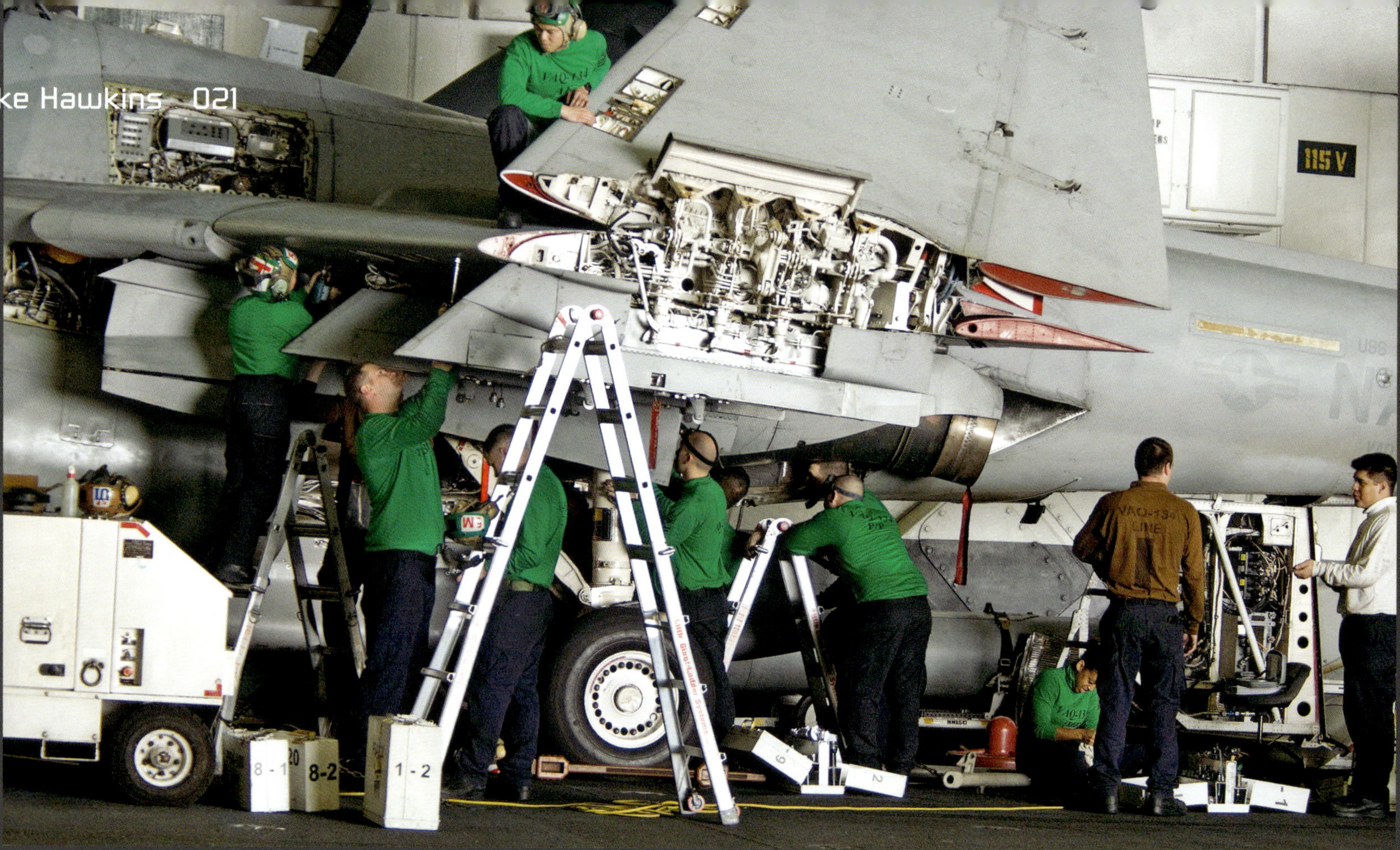

Photo: US Navy

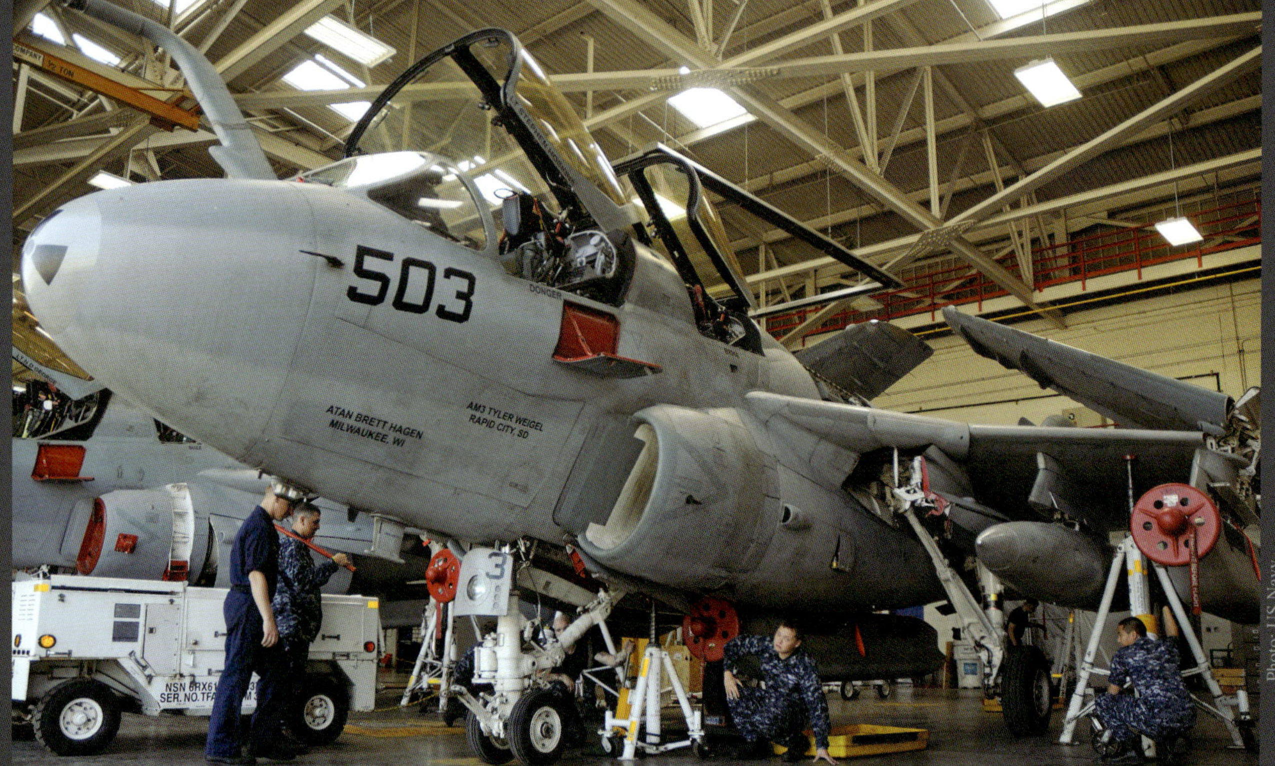

Above: This Prowler has been taken below deck for maintenance. Notice that the Central Electronics and Avionics bay panel aft of the ECMOs cockpit has been removed for checks. To the right of the photo, you can see the lowered Birdcage, or Extensible Equipment Platform, where more avionics equipment is installed. Engine covers are removed, some of the wing panels are off for inspection - I don't think this Prowler was about to fly again any time soon...

Photo: US Navy

Above: With the port engine removed, a maintenance engineer is cleaning parts of the engine bay so vital parts can be checked before the engine comes back from overhaul. Look at all the tubes and cables running throught the bay.

Right: Nighttime aboard the USS George Washinton and everything is quiet on the hangar deck. A Prowler is parked in between deck equipment, carts and a dolly with a Pratt & Whitney J52-P-408A engine. Notice the forward avionics bay door has been removed. Look at all the drop tanks hanging from the ceiling. Even though the US Navy's aircraft carriers are huge, room for 70 aircraft and all the equipment to keep them flying is restricted.

Photo: US Navy

Left: Checking the port Pratt & Whitney J-52-P-408A, looking through the main gear bay.

Below: Maintenance crew assigned to VAQ-134 perform maintenance on the starboard engine of an EA-6B Prowler in the hangar bay aboard the USS George H.W. Bush on cruise in the Atlantic Ocean in, 2013. The engine has been placed on a dolly so every part of it can be easily accessed. Look at the front end of the engine, where guide vanes can be adjusted to increase the airflow at higher engine power settings.

Pratt & Whitney J52-P-408A

The Prowler is equipped with a pair of Pratt & Whitney J-52-P-408A engines, providing the aircraft with almost 21,000 lbs of thrust. The J-52 engine was first used in the AGM-28 Hound Dog cruise missile, but the US Navy selected it for the A-6 Intruder. Since the Prowler was a derivative of the Intruder, it got the same engine, albeit from the 22nd aircraft the latter got the improved J-52-P-408A. The engine is a axial-flow dual spool turbojet with variable inlet guide vanes and air cooled turbine blades. The compressor consists of 12 stages. The Engine is rather compact at exactly 3 meters of length and a diameter of 96,5 cm. A large, curved exhaust pipe is connected to it, with a distinctive pointed down position. In the early days, the idea was to give the Intruder a movable nozzle, capable of moving down 23 degrees. This would give the aircraft Short Take Off and Landing Capabilities, but the system proved too complex and was abandonned. The Pratt & Whitney J-52-P-408A weighs 1,052 kg and requires an air mass flow of 143 lb/s.

Photo: MC3 Joshua Card, US Navy

Above: This photo shows the curved exhaust of the Pratt & Whitney J-52-P-408A engine. Look at the colours of this exhaust, which is approximately as long as the engine itself.

Left: This engine has been lifted out of the engine bay and is suspended by a cradle to allow maintenance crew to work on it. Notice the forward part of the engine is painted white. The compressor stage of the engine consists of 5 low pressure stages followed by 7 high pressure stages.

Photo: Philip Stevens

Above: "501" is an EA-6B Prowler from VAQ-130 "Zappers" - notice the small dragon on the rudder of the vertical tail. Look at the downwards angle of the engine exhaust. The exhaust pipe turns outwards and downwards, as can be seen in the photo to the right.

Right: A close-up of the port engine exhaust. Aft of the exhaust a bare metal cover protects the fuselage from the heat coming from the engine. Look at the rivets in this area. The exhaust itself is kept central by 12 metal plates linking it to the outer engine cover.

Photo: Dave Cling

Top left & left: These photos show the slightly outwards canted engine exhausts. Also look at the structure of the belly of the aircraft. The three tubes visible in the middle are an oxygen vent.

Above: The starboard engine exhaust in close-up. Look at the connection plates between the exhaust tube and the fuselage as well as the lower engine cover with the red arrows.

Left: A Prowler is being positionned on the catapult - I really like how cool the guy standing in front of the aircraft looks, as if he was looking at a painting in a museum. Notice how the aircraft's engine exhausts are pointed slightly outwards. Also interesting in this photo is the size of the main gear strut, the wing fence and the position of the horizontal tail.

Right: You better not take the warning painted above the engine exhaust for granted: not only is the blast significant, the heat is as well, with temperatures going over 400 degrees Celsius. Look at the colouring of the protective metal plate aft of the exhaust.

Below: The starboard engine exhaust, seen from above. The walkways on top of the aircraft run all the way back to the exhaust. The opening to the left is the cooling turbine exhaust for the electronic equipment located in the aft fuselage.

Below right: Looking into the port engine exhaust - see the aft part of the engine turbine all the way in the back.

Photo:Dave Clng

Photo: Akira Watanabe

Photo: Akira Watanabe

Photo: Cpl. Neysa Huertas Quinones, USMC

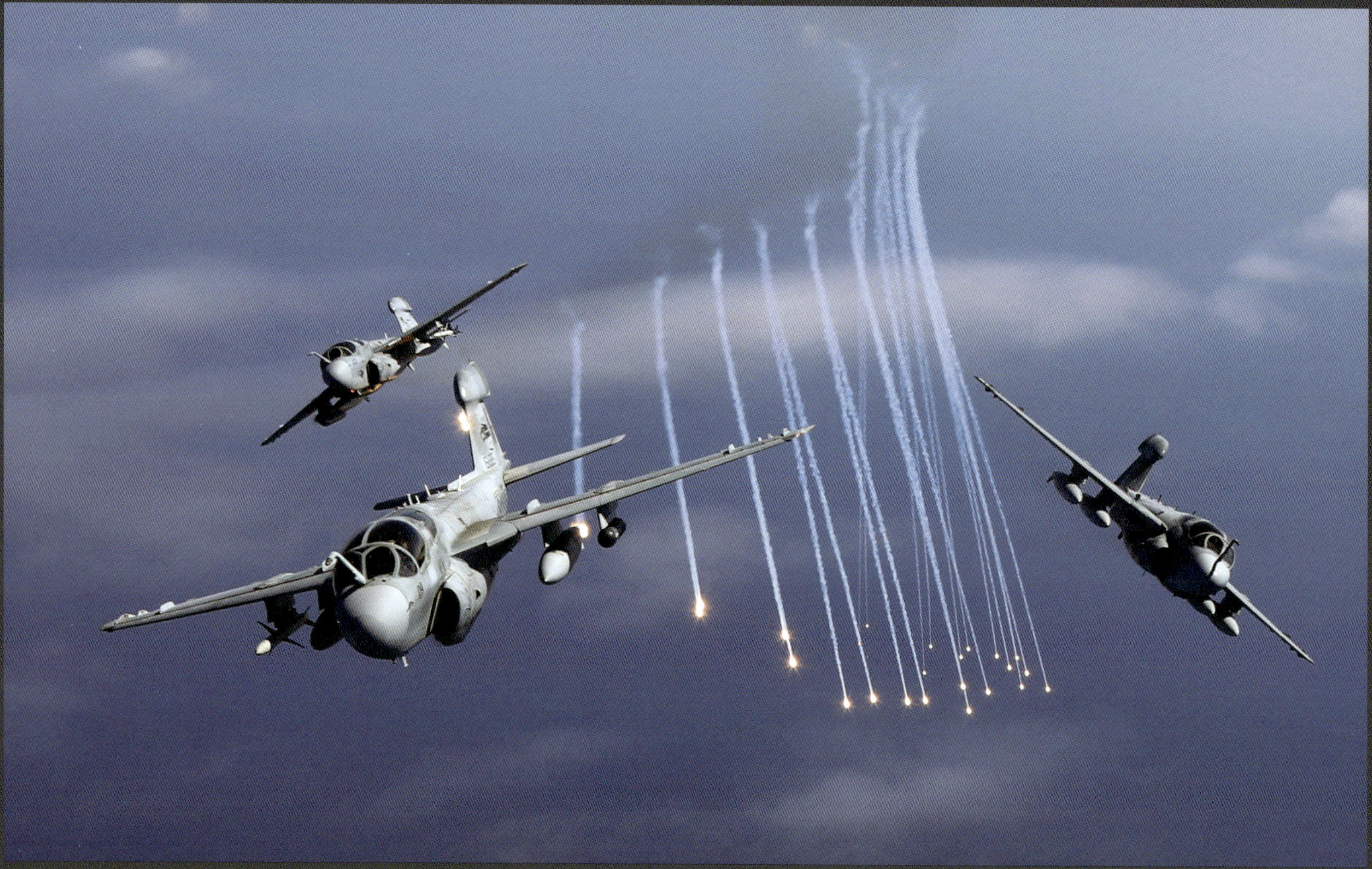

Above: Prowlers belonging to squadrons stationned at Marine Corps Air Station Cherry Point during the final flight of all units in 2016. After the flight, VMAQ-1 "Banshees" was the first to be disactivated. All 4 US Marines squadrons flying the Prowler were disactivated, with VMAQ-2 "Death Jesters" being the last, in 2019. The Prowler is equipped with flares for self defence, in case heat-seeking missiles are fired at it. Notice that the Prowler in the lead carries a HARM missile on the starboard wing and a targeting pod on the port wing. The jet to his left is loaded with 4 external droptanks.

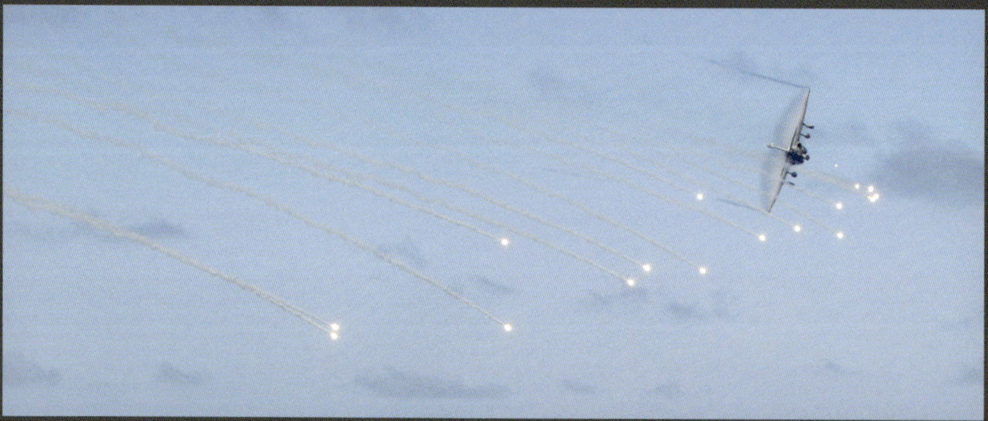

Photo: MCS Jonathan Snyder, US Navy

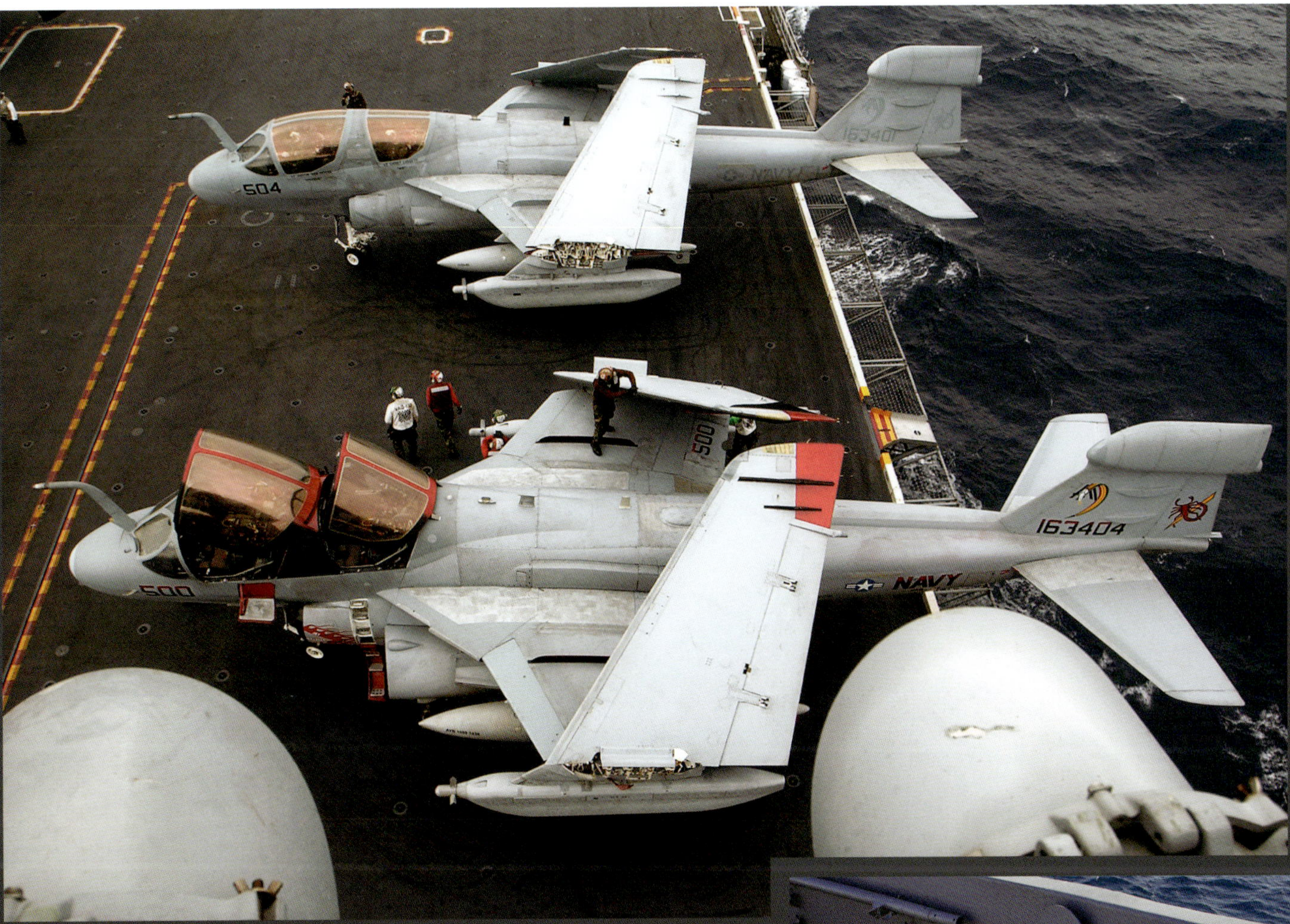

Left: Two Prowlers of VAQ-132 "Scorpions" are parked on the second starboard elevator of the USS Theodore Roosevelt. The high-viz aircraft in the front is of the CAG while the other is in low-viz. I like the black/red framing on the gold-tinted canopies. An interesting detail is on the ship's edge, to depose of explosives... The photo below shows a similar area in detail.

End of the story

The final flight of the Grumman EA-6B Prowler ended in the spring of 2019, when a jet of VMAQ-2 "Death Jesters" landed for the last time. The US Navy started withdrawing the type from its inventory as early as 2009, with the last three squadrons, VAQ-131 "Lancers", VAQ-134 "Garudas" and VAQ-142 Gray Wolves" turning in their jets in 2015. All of the 15 Prowler squadrons active have since transitionned to the EA-18G Growler and all but one are stationned at NAS Whidbey Island in the northwest of Washington state. The exception is VAQ-141 "Shadowhawks", which is based at MCAS Iwakuni, in the south of Japan.

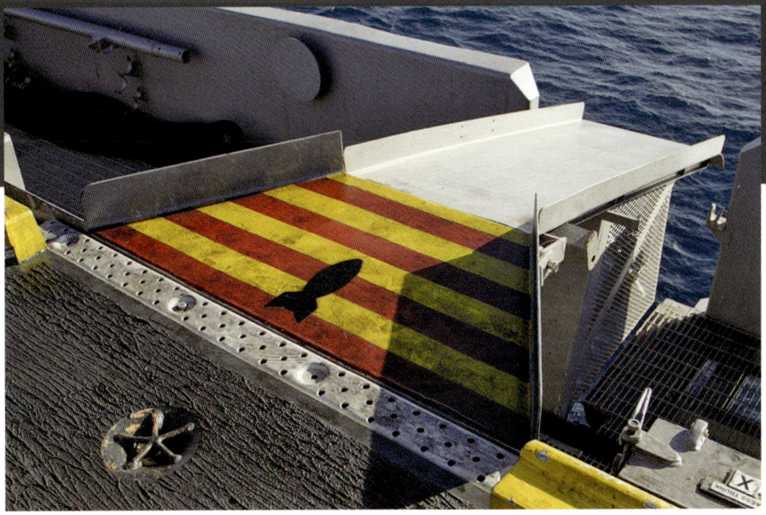

Photo: Stephan Ortmann

External loads

The classic lay-out of the Grumman EA-6B Prowler are three electronic pods
and a pair of external fuel tanks, similar to the aircraft in the photo above, on
final approach towards the carrier. There are however variations in the lay-out
of the ordnance and we'll go over these in these pages. The Prowler can be
used in a completely offensive way by being loaded with one or two AGM-88
HARM High-Speed Anti Radiation missiles, which are used against enemy
radar systems.

Photo: Akira Watanabe

Left: Have a closer look at this Prowler of VMAQ-3 "Moondogs" coming in to land at MCAS Yuma. It is loaded with an AN/AAQ-28(V) LITENING targeting pod. The pod gave the Prowlers ECMOs - Electronic Countermeasures Officers - a video picture that enabled them to observe Improvised Explosive Devices on the ground in Iraq and Afghanistan and to better employ the Prowler's jammers to disrupt the remote detonation signals coming from cellphones.

Above: A closer look at the centerline station, looking forward.

Right: Not an every day configuration for a Prowler, is the ACMI pod that is fixed to the inboard starboard pylon. ACMI stands for Air Combat Manoeuvering Instrumentation, which is something the aircraft probably isn't all that familiar with...

Photo: David Draycott

Photo: Stephan Ortmann

The primary load for the EA-6B is the ALQ-99 jammer pod, of which usually three are carried. These pods can jam a wide range of overlapping frequency bands, from Band 1 - VHF - to band 10 - Ku - which is in the microwave range of frequencies from 12 to 18 gigahertz. Each pod has a control computer linked to the ALQ-99 Central Processing Unit - CPU - on the aircraft. This CPU processes the received threat signals, displays them for the ECMOs in the aft cockpit and manages the jamming of the signal. The Prowler has a 360 degree coverage; the receivers in the blisters on the side of the vertical tail house the antennas for VHF and VHF/UHF - bands 1 and 2 - while the receivers in the football on top of the tail receive higher frequency bands.

Photo: Dave Ching

Below: The ALQ-99 jammer pods are open at the back, while the front has a RAM turbine, which provides electricity to the jammer and transmitters inside the pod. The ALQ-99 weighs some 440 kg.

Photo: Dave Chng

Right: The AN/ALQ-99 Electronic Warfare System is what made the Prowler such an important asset to the US Navy and US Marines. The system consists of the Jamming pods for transmitting and the Footbal on top of the vertical tail and the blisters on either side of it for receiving. These photos show the jammer pods in detail, with the Ram Air Turbine at the front prominent. On the trailing edge of the outer pylon, a navigation light is located, as can be seen in the photo below right.

Photo: Dave Clng

Photo: Dave Clng

Photo: Dave Clng

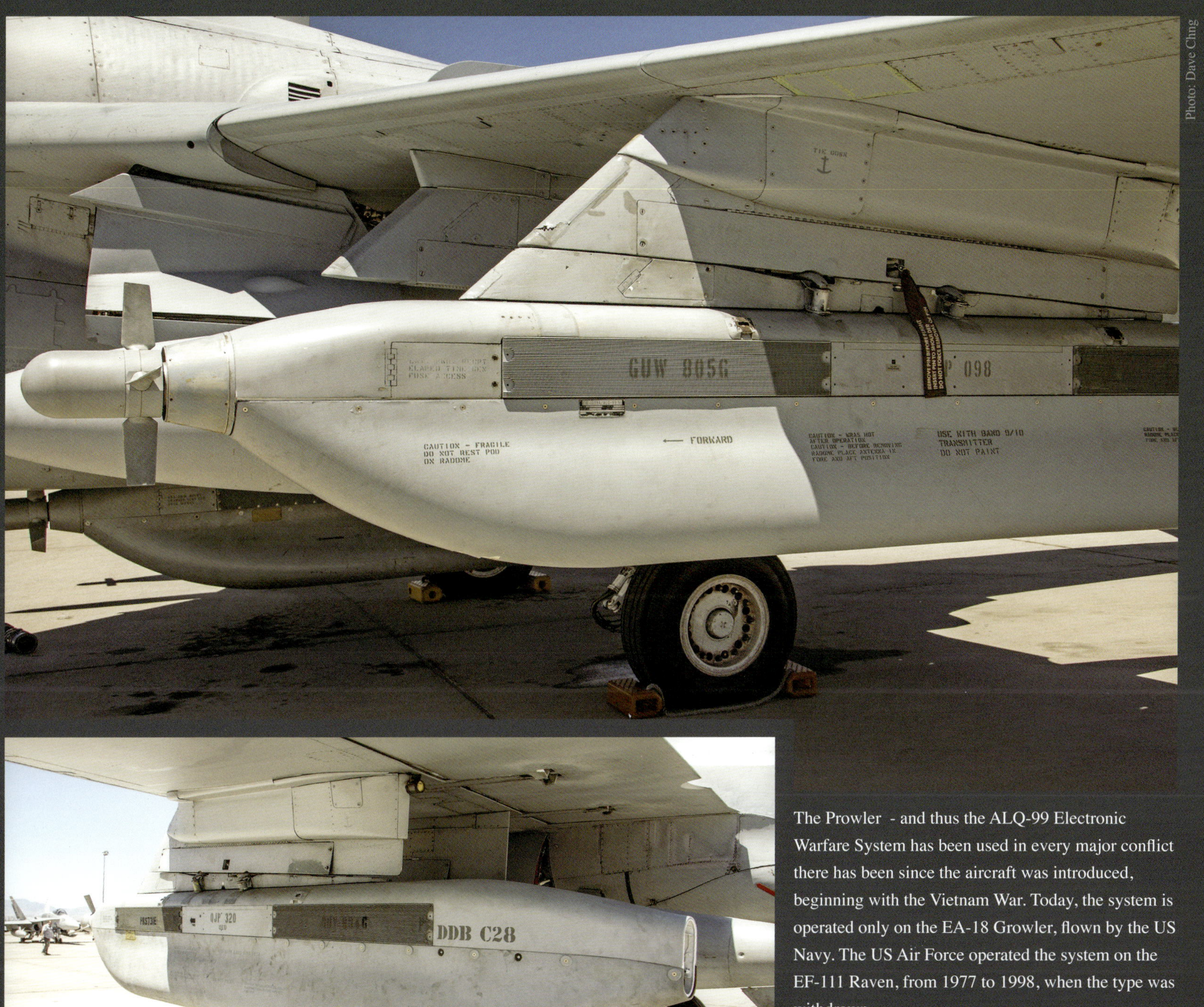

Photo: Dave Cing

Photo: Dave Cing

The Prowler - and thus the ALQ-99 Electronic Warfare System has been used in every major conflict there has been since the aircraft was introduced, beginning with the Vietnam War. Today, the system is operated only on the EA-18 Growler, flown by the US Navy. The US Air Force operated the system on the EF-111 Raven, from 1977 to 1998, when the type was withdrawn.

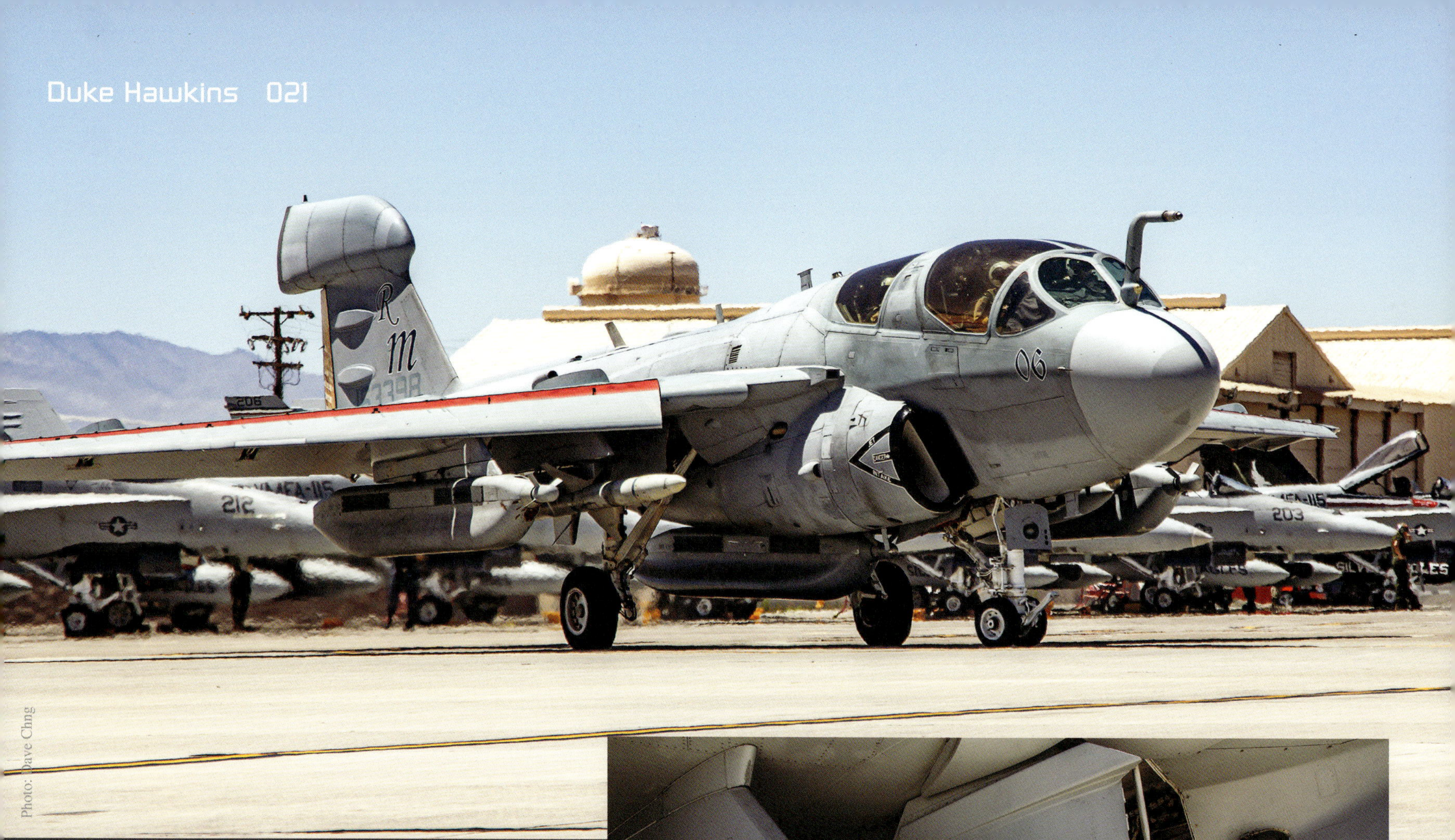

Photo: Dave Chng

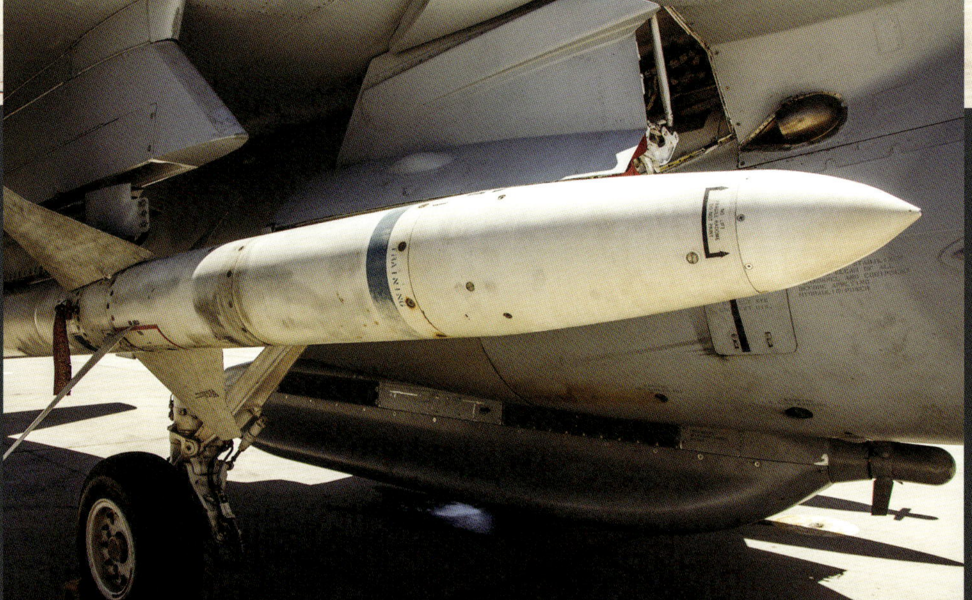

Above: The ICAP II upgrade introduced the Prowler with the capability to fire the AGM-88 HARM - High Speed Anti-Radiation Missile.

Below: This Prowler carries two pairs of external fuel tanks.

Photo: Dave Chng

Photo: Dave Chng

Above: The AGM-88 is a formidable weapon, used to detect and destroy radar antennas or transmitters. Once a target is located, the missile can home in on it, even if that target stops transmitting. With a range of over 100 km, the aircraft firing the missile can stay at a safe distance. The AGM-88 weighs 355 kg, has a length of 4.1 meter and a cost of nearly 300,000 US$.

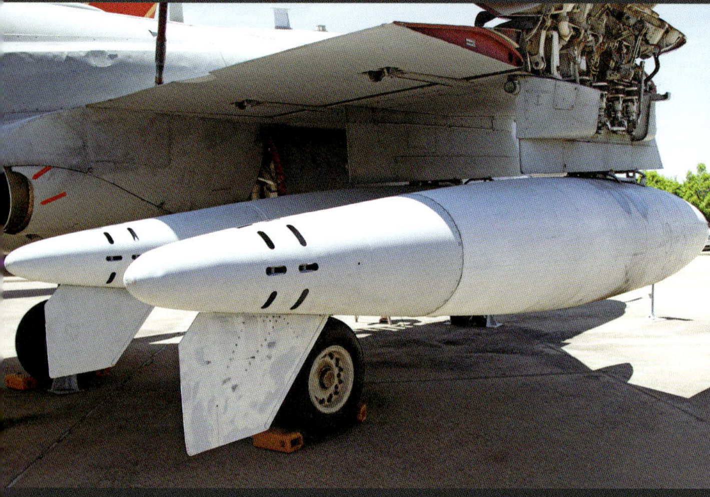

Photo: MCS3 Ryan Mayes, US Navy

Photo: Dave Cling

Above: Fall 2012 and an EA-6B Prowler assigned to the "Gray Wolves" of VAQ-142 is readied for takeoff onboard the aircraft carrier USS Nimitz. On the outboard pylon, it carries an AGM-88 HARM. Look at the position of the ECMO's head in the back cockpit. Looks like he's ready for the catapult shot...

Left: The HARM is fixed on a pylon adapter - the head of the missile is to the right. When a HARM is fired, the pilot calls "Magnum", in the same way that fighter pilot call "Fox 1" or "Fox 2" when they fire a radar guided missile or a heat seeking missile respectively.

Photo: Joe Copalman

Prowler Action !

Time for some Prowler action! The photo above shows a US Marines Prowler being refuelled. Look at the weathering on the fuselage and how dark the canopies are tinted. The photo to the right shows just how hard the job of a naval aviator actually can be. Landing on a ship, filled with parked aircraft on every side. Precision, timing, speed; they all have to be just perfect. The flaps and hook are down, the speed brakes are open. With the help of the LSO, in a few seconds, this EA-6B will be on the deck.

Photo: US Navy

Right: Taking off for another mission in the Persian Gulf in the fall of 2014. The Prowler, part of VAQ-134 "Garudas" operated from the USS George H.W. Bush during the final deployment of the unit on the type. After returning, it would take until 2016 before the squadron took delivery of the EA-18 Growler. The rudder shows the squadron logo, refering to a Garuda, which is a creature half human, half eagle.

Photo: MCS 3rd Class Joshua Card, US Navy

Photo: MCS Aiyana Paschal, US Navy

Above: A Super Hornet of the "Argonauts" is refuelling a Prowler of the "Gray Wolves" during a training flight of the USS Nimitz in 2013. The Super Hornet is used in a large variety of roles and I have to say, it looks pretty cool in the refuelling role, with all the external fuel tanks!

Photo: Philip Stevens

Photo: MCS-Chris Bartlett, US Navy

Photo: Stephan Ortmann

Left: Moments after having caught the wire aboard the USS Nimitz, this "Gray Wolf" is folding its wings to take as little as space as possible. Look at the position of the nose landing gear. On the starboard inboard pylon, an AGM-88 HARM is carried.

Top: A Prowler of the "Shadowhawks" is about to catch the wire aboard the USS Theodore Roosevelt. Notice the lowered arrestor hook and the deployed speed brakes.

Above: These metal curved brackets are used to keep the wires off the deck, so that the arrestor hooks of the aircraft can catch them. Notice the tie down point - these are located all over the deck.

Left: Aboard the USS Harry S. Truman, a Prowler of VAQ-130 "Zappers" is putting its wings down. While one Super Hornet is about to blast of the nr. 4 catapult, another one is already waiting its turn, loaded with a smart bomb. It's always busy on the deck of an aircraft carrier.

Below: Lots of activity on the tarmac of Nellis during Red Flag. Behind the pair of Prowlers, you can spot a Super Hornet, an F-16 and lots of F-15 Eagles.

Photo: US Navy

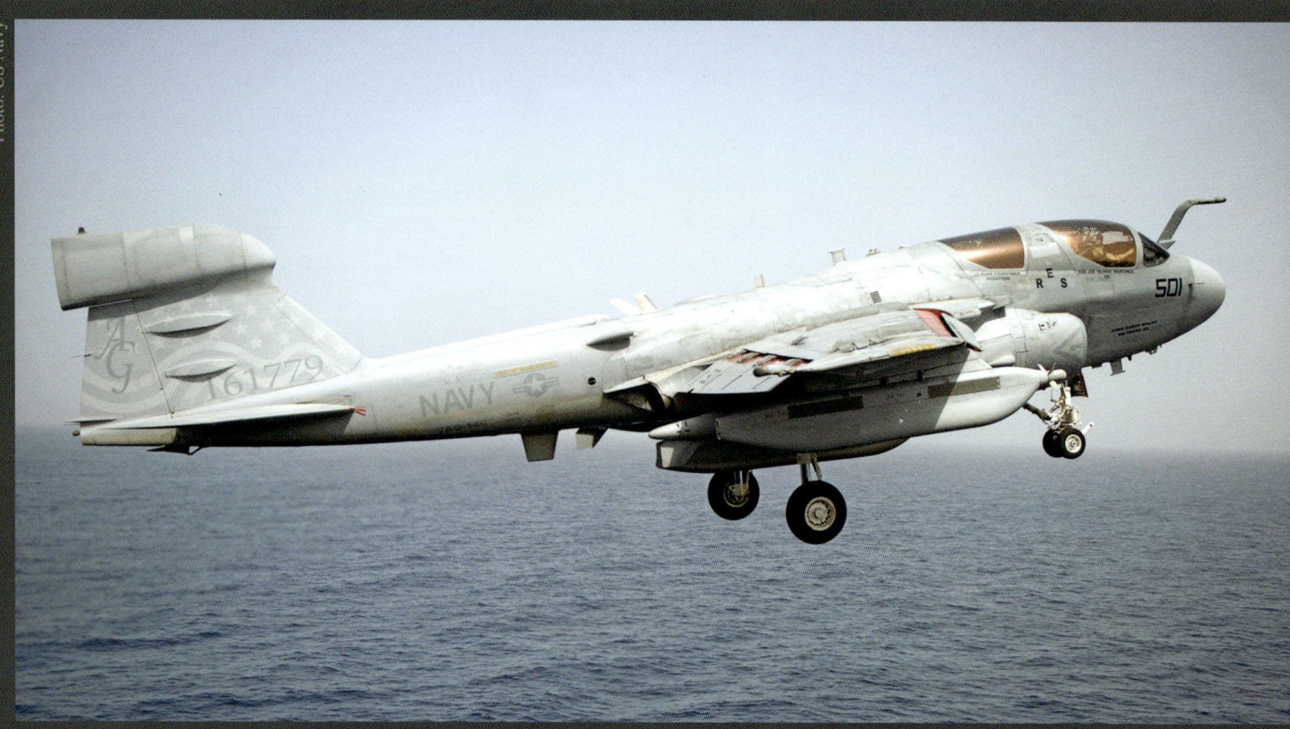

Left: Sporting a low viz American flag on the vertical tail, this Prowler of VAQ-140 "Patriots" is taking off from the port catapult of the USS Dwight D. Eisenhower. Notice the R, E and S on the forward fuselage. These are service ribbons: E is an award for battle efficiency, S for safety and R for the Admiral Arthur W. Radford Award, which is given to the best electronic attack squadron in the US Navy.

Below: 06 of VMAQ-4 "Seahawks" carries both high viz and low viz markings.

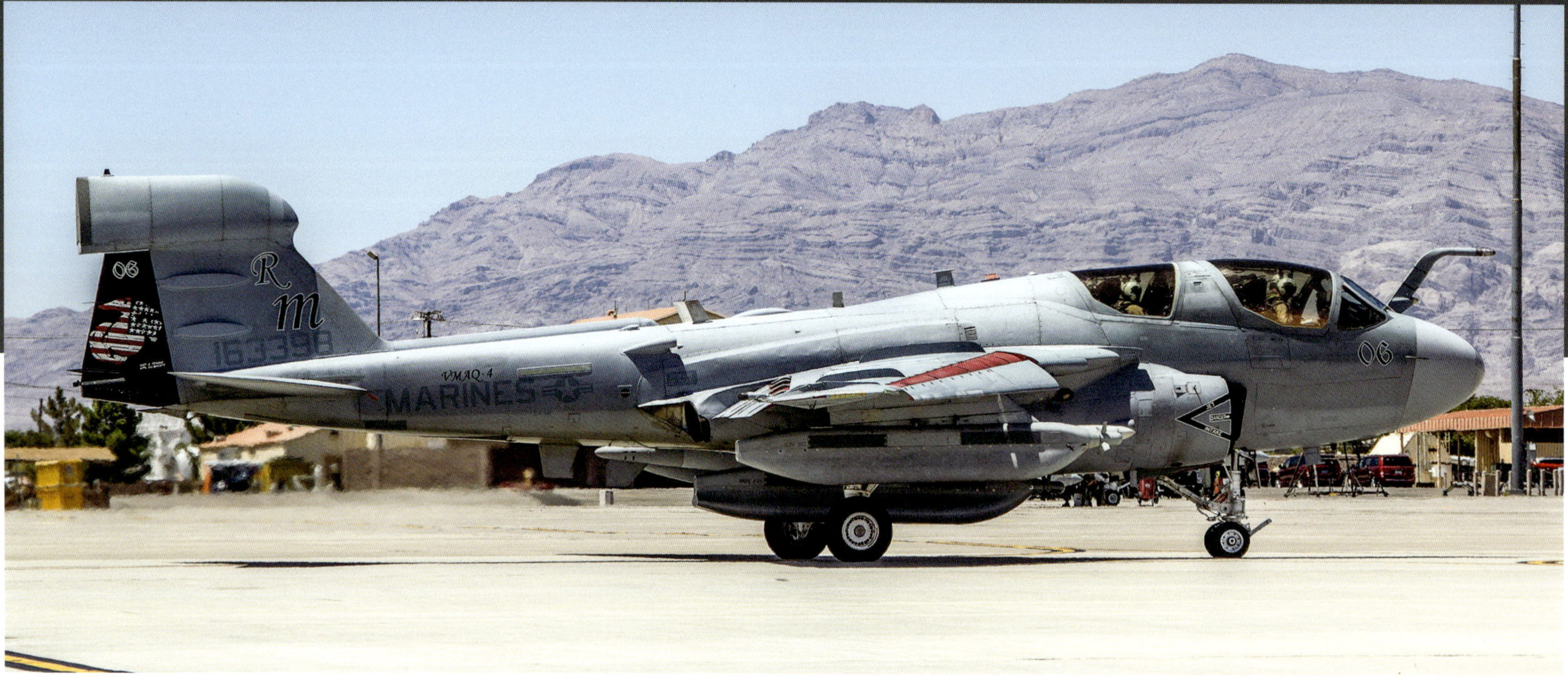

Photo: Dave Chng

Photo: Dave Chng

Taking off at a steep angle, this jet of VAQ-129 "Vikings" shows just how agile a Prowler can be. Look at the completely lowered leading edge slats and the position of the trailing edge flaps. "900" is loaded with three external fuel tanks, each providing over a 1,000 liters of additional fuel. Notice that the tank on the centerline pylon doesn't have a vertical fin mounted, like the two others have. Another awesome shot from Dave Chng.

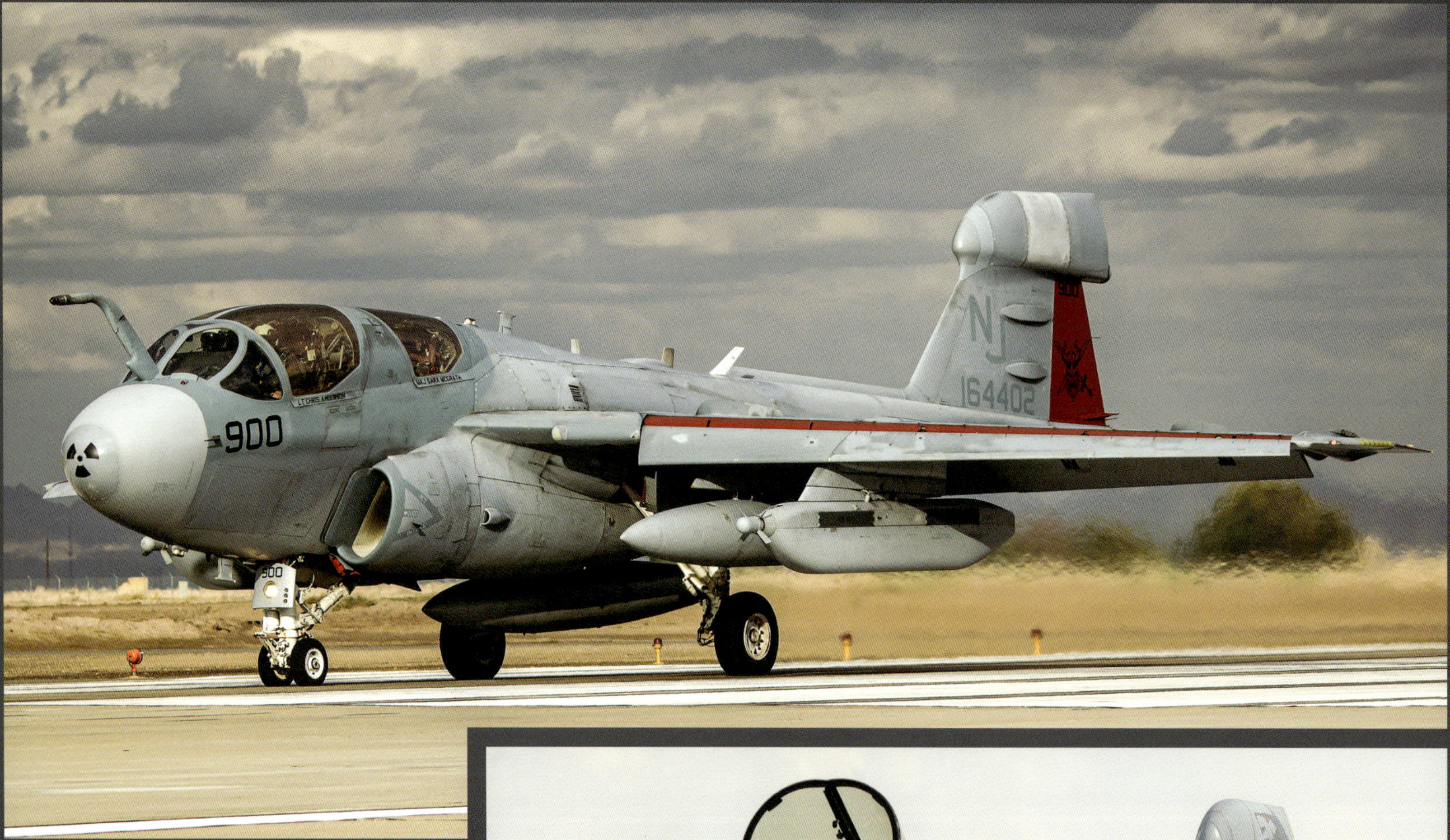

Photo: Dave Ching

Above: VAQ-129 "Vikings" is on the runway, ready for take off. Some interesting details in this photo: the red rudder, different colours of panels and the much lighter shade of the radome.

Photo: Andreas Zeitler

Right: A Prowler of VMAQ-3 passes in front of the public at an airshow at NAS Oceana in 2004. The unit, nicknamed "Moon Dogs" was decommissioned in 2018 when the type was withdrawn from service. The logo on the tail reminds me of the one carried by the F-16s of the 8th Fighter Wing "Wolf Pack" flying out of Kunsan Air Base in Korea. I've checked it out and there is a slight difference...

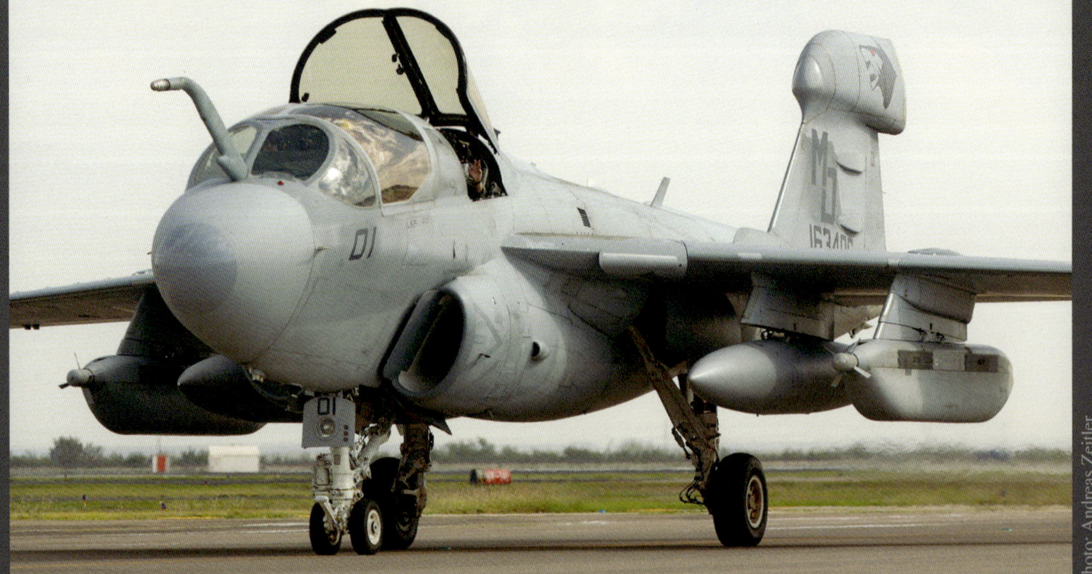

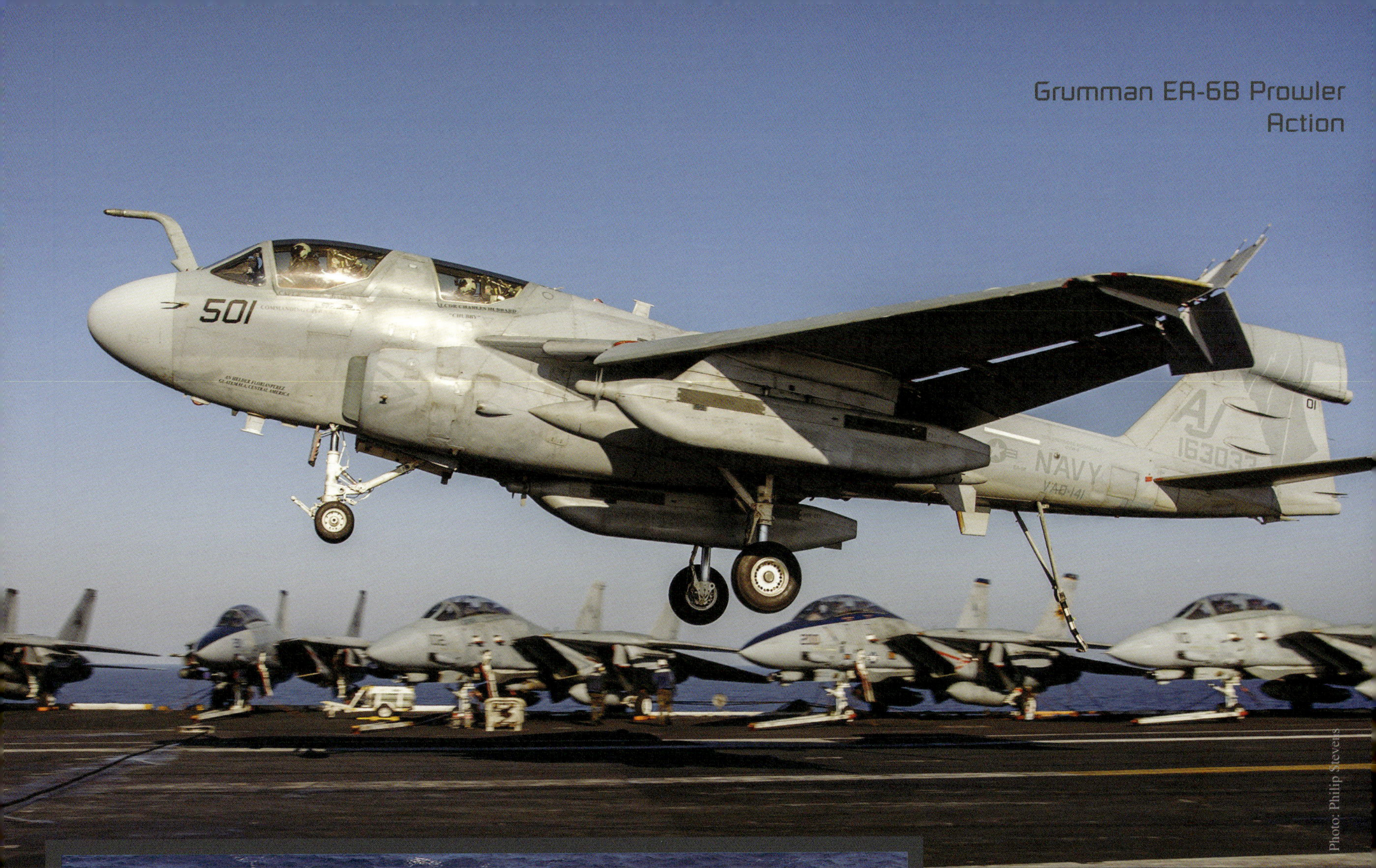

Above: A Prowler of VAQ-141 "Shadowhawks" is about to land on the USS Theodore Roosevelt. Look at the lowered arrestor hook and open speed brakes near the wing tip. In the background, 5 Super Tomcats are parked. The photo was taken during the last cruise of the F-14.

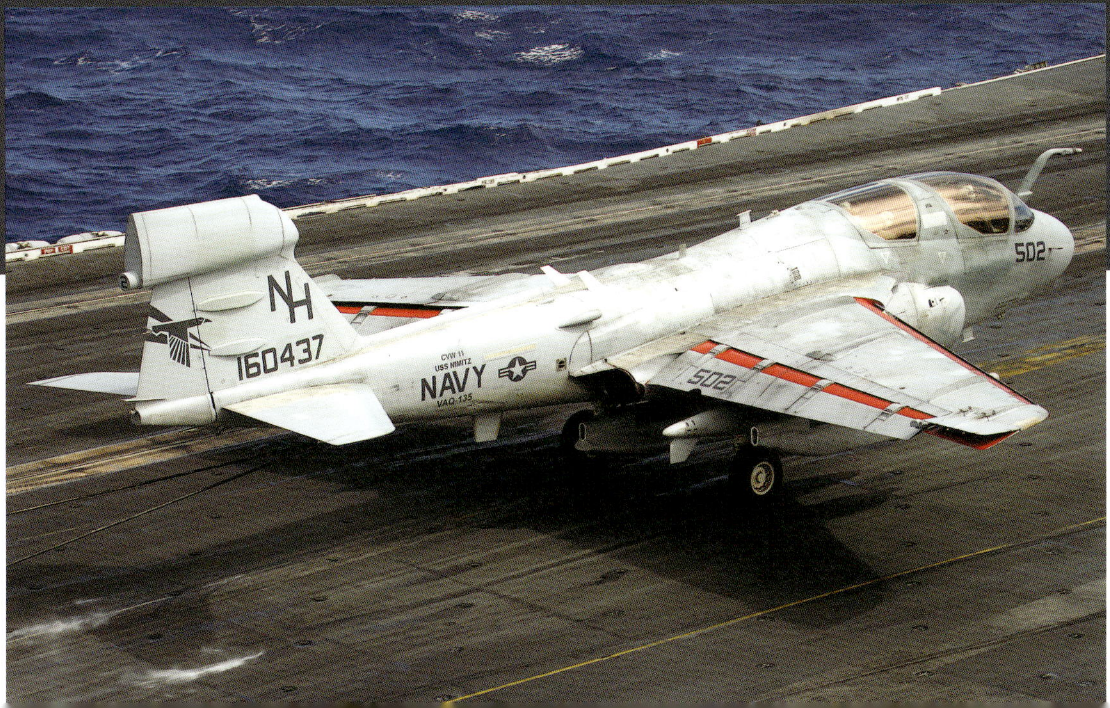

Left: 502 of the "Black Ravens" has caught the wire aboard the USS Nimitz after a mission in the Gulf. Look how weathered the top side of the aircraft is. The unit can trace its history back to May 1969, when it was tasked to provide Electronic Warfare and Aerial Refuelling, flying the Douglas EKA-3B Skywarrior.

Above: Fall 2012 aboard the USS Dwight D. Eisenhower during Operation Enduring Freedom. A Prowler of VAQ-140 "Patriots"is waiting for the deflector doors to lower and take position on the port bow catapult. In front of it, an E-2C Hawkeye of VAW-121 "Bluetails" is launched.

Right: A very cool looking Darth Vader is painted on the tail of this high-viz "Star Warrior" of VAQ-209. The unit is a US Navy Reserve Squadron that was established in 1977, flying the EA-6A Intruder. In 1990, it transitionned to the EA-6B, which it continued to fly for 23 years. In 2014, VAQ-209 began flying the EA-18G Growler.

Photo: MCSS Sabrina Fine, US Navy

Photo: Kevin Whitehead

Right: A mixed instructor/student crew with VAQ-129 prepares to depart NAF El Centro for a night training sortie in February 2014. As the 'Vikings' ceased training new EA-6B aircrews the following month, this proved to be VAQ-129's final detachment to El Centro. Look at the landing light located in the nose wheel gear door.

Below: This photo taken on board the USS Harry S. Truman, shows a colourful Prowler of VAQ-130 "Zappers" parked at the "point" of the deck, in front of the forward elevator. Look how close the legacy Hornet is parked to the edge of the deck behind it. To the left, another Hornet is lowering its wings moments before being catapulted from the starboard bow catapult.

Photo: Joe Copalman

Photo: Stephan Ortmann

Photo: Kevin Whitehead

Above: An ICAP II Prowler of VAQ-135 "Black Ravens" is about to land aboard the USS Nimitz, back in 2005. Look at the special livery with droopy looking eyes. This aircraft was lost a few months after this photo was taken, when it crashed in Oregon, just south of the state border with Washington. One of its engines failed during a low level training mission. Fortunately, all 4 crew members ejected safely.

Right: Brown 530 of VAQ-133 "Wizards" during Red Flag.

Photo: Kevin Whitehead

Photo: Stephan Ortmann

Above: Steam is coming from one of the port side catapults while a Prowler is about to line up with it. Look at the position of the leading edge flaps.

Right: A very cool looking Prowler of VMAQ-1 "Banshees". After the first Gulf War, it was decided to reorganise the three Electronic Warfare Squadrons of the Marines and form a fourth. This resulted in the activation in 1992 of VMAQ-1; a unit which would fly the Prowler until in was disactivated in 2016. The spoilers on the aircraft's wings are lifted.

Photo: Kevin Whitehead

Top: The plane captain - which is like a naval crew chief - is cleaning the forward canopy of his Prowler before the flight crew arrives. The jet is hooked up to ground power and wheels chocks keep the aircraft in its place.

Left: Wheel chocks are placed near the base of a cable retainer.

Above: Equipment for the aircraft is carried around the flight deck in these two-wheel carts. This one is filled with flares refils.

Photo: Stefan Darte

Above: While a fully loaded F-16 of the Belgian Air Force patiently waits its turn to get some much needed juice, an EA-6B Prowler of VAQ-131 is being fueled up, somewhere over the Middle East. Notice how the KC-135, originally based at McConnell Air Force Base in Wichita, Kansas has the capacity to provide fuel to both systems of air-to-air refuelling: probe or receptacle. The Prowler is from Electronic Attack Squadron 131, Lancers. The unit with callsign "Skybolt" can track its history back to 1946 when it was established as Patrol Squadron 931, flying on the P2V Neptune. In 1956 the squadron transitionned to the A-3 Skywarrior, an aircraft with which it flew many missions in the Vietnam War between 1963 and 1968. Transition to the EA-6B Prowler began in 1971. The squadron was one of the most experienced ones on the type, which it continued to operate for 43 years. After such a long career, the Prowlers were taken out of service and replaced by Super Hornet based Growlers. Today, the Lancers are one of the many squadrons flying the Growler that have their home base at Naval Air Station Whidbey Island near Oak Harbor, Washington state.

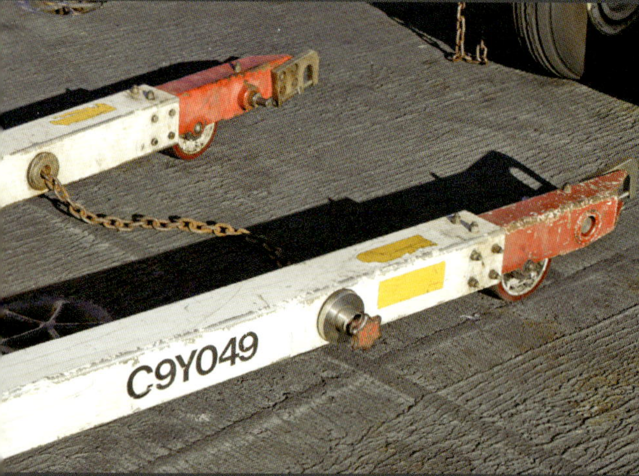

Photo: Stephan Ortmann

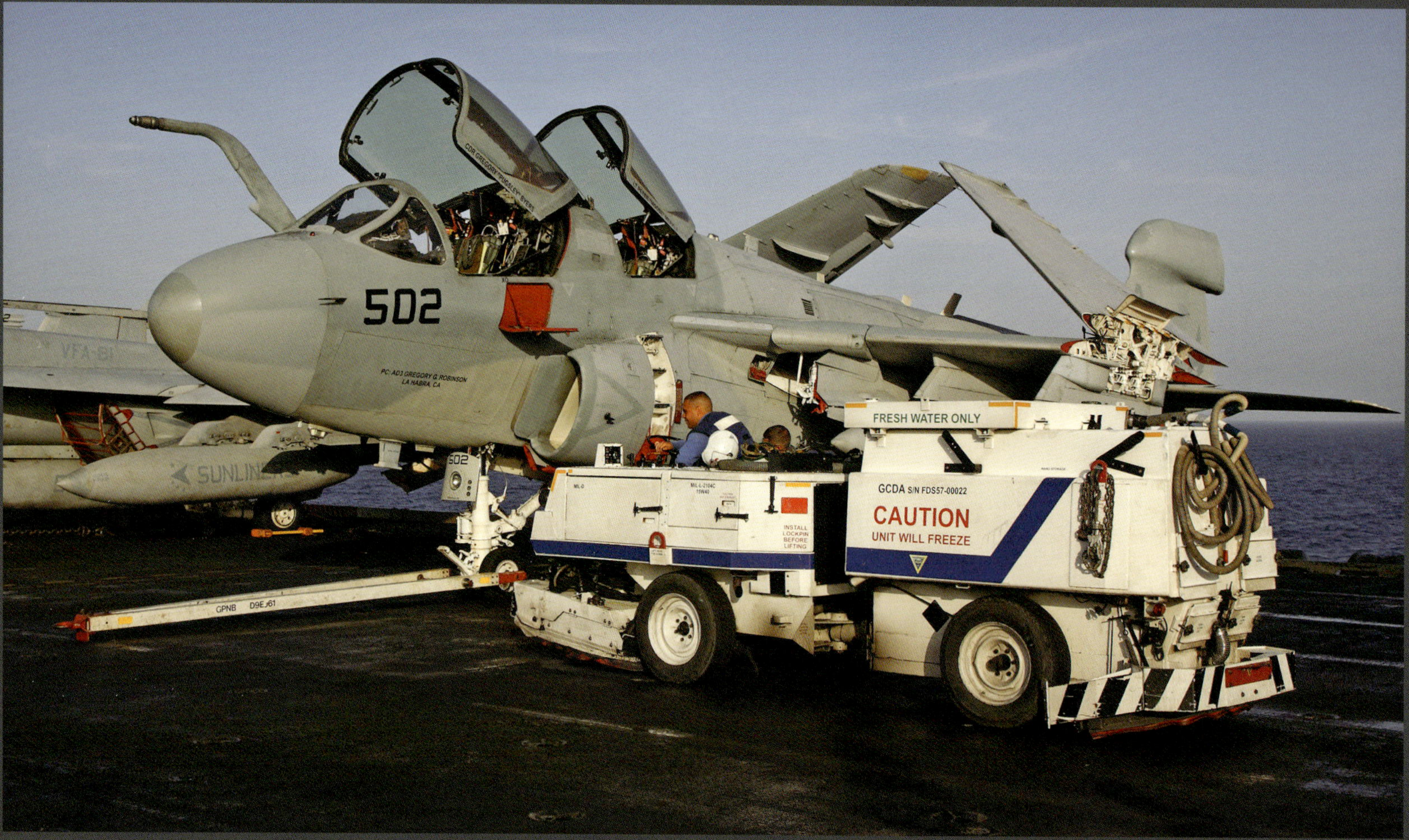

Photo: Stephan Ortmann

Photo: Stephan Ortmann

Above: Early morning and the deck is being cleaned before the flight operations start. The canopies of this prowler have already been cleaned and the jet waits for the crew to arrive. The towbar is still fixed to the nose wheel.

Opposite page: Deck crew are about to fix a towbar to a prowler of VAQ-136. Notice the details of the boarding ladder and the cockpit framing.

Left: Close-ups of the tow bar.

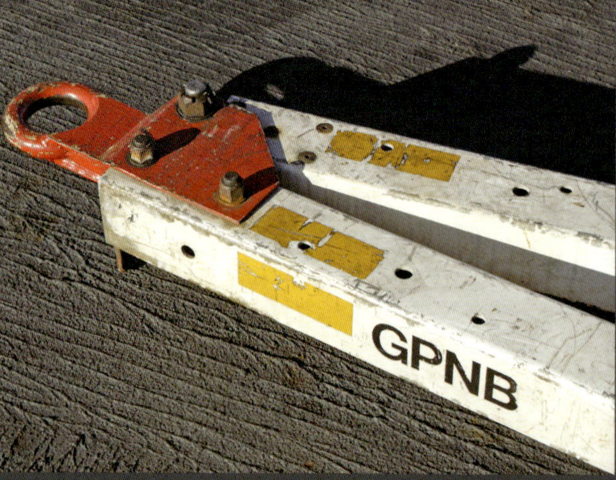

Grumman EA-6B Prowler
Action
500
"MAGWAI" CAG
LT MICHAEL WHITE
LTJG BE
"LUNC
WARNING
GPNB
C9Y048
JET
DANGER
Photo: Stephan Ortmann
133

Above: A cart placed close to the aircraft carrier's island is filled with equipment and flares for one of the Prowlers of VAQ-136 Gauntlets. Each unit has its own equipment carts assigned, to make sure every type receives the correct amount and type of equipment.

Above: The deck crew aboard the USS George Washington takes a break in between flight operations. Notice the tractor used to tow the aircraft around on the deck. In the background, an F/A-18F Super Hornet and an EA-6B of the Gauntlets is parked. It's actually the same aircraft as the one in the photo on the opposite page.

Right: A Prowler of VAQ-136 Gauntlets is being towed to its parking spot next to the forward elevator - notice the crew chief in the pilot's seat - while another EA-6B is about to be launched of the starboard catapult. Look how far the aft fuselages hangs over the edge of the deck. On the port side of the flight deck, Super Hornets are parked.

NAVY
500
164402
USS GEORGE WASHINGTON
503
503

Left: So, technically, there's a Prowler in this photo, but I thought it might interest the modellers among you for the details on the inside structure of the deflection doors of the catapult. The system is built up out of 6 vertical doors, each pushed up by means of two actuators. Two deck crew are fixing a strut to the first door so that the mechanism can be checked. Look at the weathering of some of the doors, the edges of which are painted red and white striped.

Below: A close-up of the shuttle pulling the aircraft to the edge of the deck. The catapults on Nimitz class carriers are steam operated, the Gerald R. Ford-class ships will have a Electromagnetic Aircraft Launch System.

Above: This photo shows the details on the lower part of the deflection door mechanism. The insides are painted white, with the edges in yellow.

Left: A Prowler is directed towards one of the bow catapults. Once past the deflector doors, they are lifted to protect the deck crew and aircraft behind the jet. Notice the detail of the launch rail where the shuttle pulls the aircraft to the edge of the ship.

Below: The front part of the launch rail where the shuttle is fixed and the aircraft hooked up. The edges of the launch rail are painted yellow.

Photo: Stephan Ortmann

Photo: USMC

Duke
Hawkins

If you have this book in your hands, chances are high that you are, like me, an aircraft enthusiast. And when iconic aircraft are taken out of service, it always leaves a strange feeling. That was definitely the case in 2019 when the Prowler was retired from service with the US Marines, after a career of nearly 50 years. It motivated us to include the aircraft in our series of photograhic portraits and here it finally is. In a time where most missions aboard US aircraft carriers are done by a single type, I look back in melancholy on the times when the flight decks of aircraft carriers were filled with Tomcats, Prowlers, Hornets, Vikings, Greyhounds, Hawkeyes and Seahawks. Remember those days?

The 4-seat Prowler has been widely used and was a witness in many conflicts, starting with the Vietnam War all the way to the air war over Syria. For this book we gathered the photos of talented photographers from around the world. We owe them a big thank you and look forward in realising more projects in the near future. I also want to thank you, our reader, for the feedback that you give us, the suggestions and the enthusiasm to continue the series. It is extremely motivating and we really hope to hear even more from you! I hope you enjoyed this book and for the modellers among you: don't hesitate to send us photos of your models!

Duke